INSIDE

ULTIMATE PLAYER 38

2017...
THE YEAR OF THE POG!

What does 2017 hold for the MAN. UNITED megastar?

BONKERS BARNETS

THE AFRO? THE TOP KNOT? THE CORN ROWS?

BALLON D'OR BATTLE

FOOTBALL'S KING OF COOL

TROPHY TIME

POGBA 4

THE KING OF LA LIGA! ★ THE KING OF LA LIGA! ★ THE KING OF LA LIGA!

LIONEL MESSI

ROUTE TO THE THRONE

5 BALLONS D'OR
Nobody has been named the world's best player as many times as Messi!

WEAPONS ARMOURY
- Creative Genius
- Deadly Dribbling
- Lethal Finishing

91
In 2012, Messi broke the record for goals scored in a calendar year!

TROPHY CABINET

ROYAL MOMENTS!

KING OF EUROPE | SIX OF THE BEST | GOALSCORING KING | TRIO'S TREBLE

KINGS OF EUROPE – MESSI 22

STARS' CARS!

Check out the speed machines top footy stars drive!

MEMPHIS
ROONEY
ROLLS ROYCE PHANTOM
BMW i8
POGBA
ALVES
BENTLEY CONTINENTAL GTC
MASERATI GRANTURISMO
FERRARI FF
CLYNE
MERCEDES G 63 AMG
DE BRUYNE
LAMBORGHINI AVENTADOR
SANCHEZ

STARS' CARS 24

FIFA THROUGH THE AGES

The introduction of 'The Journey' in FIFA 17 is one of the biggest additions EA have ever made! Check out some of the other major changes to the game over the years.

FIRST-EVER GAME | ALL THE LEAGUES | CAREER MODE
CLUB TEAMS
REAL PLAYERS
SOUNDTRACK
BE A PRO
ONLINE
THE JOURNEY
ULTIMATE TEAM

FIFA THROUGH THE AGES 62

2017... THE YEAR OF THE POG!

What does 2017 hold for the MAN. UNITED megastar?

PAUL POGBA is one of the biggest names in world footy right now! MATCH checks out what could be in store for footy's most expensive player this year...

TROPHY TIME

Pog is used to winning things – since leaving Man. United he's won four Serie A titles and two Coppa Italias! Now he's back at Old Trafford, he'll be desperate to add to his trophy cabinet – and fast!

MY MIDDLE NAME IS 'COOL'!

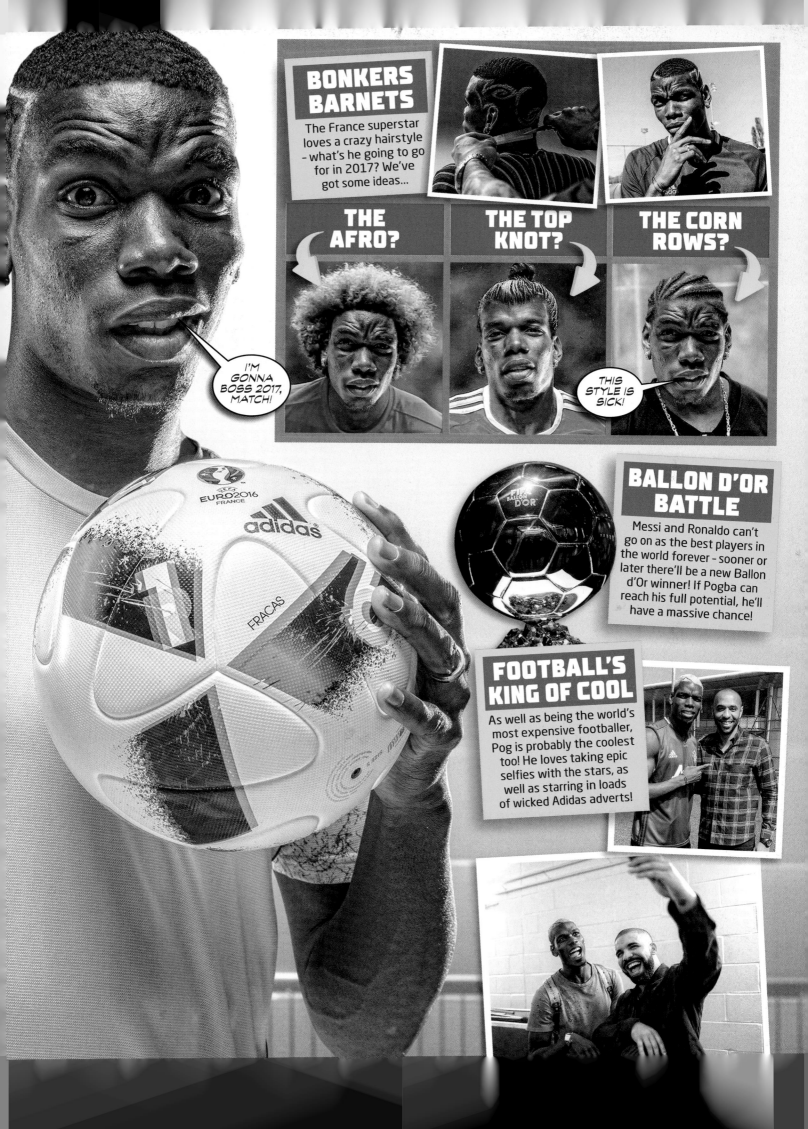

TURE XI!

RUBEN LOFTUS-CHEEK

Loftus-Cheek has been on the fringes of Chelsea's first team for a couple of seasons now, but we think 2017 could be his breakthrough year! His eye for a pass is top quality!

ERIC DIER

MARCUS RASHFORD

DEMARAI GRAY

We reckon the Leicester man has a huge future! He's got bags of flair and has impressed for the U21s, too - that's why we picked him over players like Sterling and Oxlade-Chamberlain!

YOUR SHOUT!

Tell us who would be in your future England XI on the MATCH Facebook page!

HOME NATIONS HEROES!

We're backing these youngsters to make a big impact at Euro 2020, too!

PADDY McNAIR
NORTHERN IRELAND CENTRE-BACK

The Sunderland young gun can play in defence or midfield, and will definitely be at Euro 2020 if Northern Ireland qualify!

REGAN POOLE
WALES CENTRE-BACK

Man. United have big hopes for this guy! He's really calm on the ball, and could be key for Wales in the future. Watch this space!

CALLUM O'DOWDA
REPUBLIC OF IRELAND WINGER

Bristol City paid over £1 million to land this guy this summer, and Martin O'Neill has said the skilful wide man is the future of Irish footy!

RYAN GAULD
SCOTLAND WINGER

Sporting paid £3 million to sign 'The Scottish Messi' from Dundee in 2014, and the epic dribbler could be a big star in Portugal!

STAR WARS
FOOTY VILLAINS

The release of Rogue One: A Star Wars Story got MATCH thinking about which footy stars have gone over to the Dark Side!

MY ACCURACY IS CLASS!

LUIS SUAREZ IS...
BOBA FETT
The sharp shooter hunts down defenders and never gives up on his prey! He's a great weapon when he's on your side, but you'd hate to be up against him! You know you're in a scrap when Luis is about!

BEEP BOOP!

DIEGO COSTA IS...
KYLO REN
His master Mourinho has left him, but Costa still has evil in him! The striker wreaks tons of havoc at The Bridge with his massive temper and full-blooded tackles, and he doesn't care who gets in his way!

THIS SUIT'S WELL HEAVY!

JOSE MOURINHO IS...
DARTH VADER

Jose started out as a good guy at Porto, but he's become evil since he got more power! The legendary manager wants to have control over everybody – his players, referees and opponents – in a bid to rule the galaxy!

DON'T MESS WITH US!

PEPE & RAMOS ARE...
STORMTROOPERS

Dressed in white, these battlers carry out their team's dirty work! They're absolutely ruthless in destroying their enemies, and they'll do whatever it takes to defeat their opponent! They stop at nothing!

FOOTY FAMILIES!

Did you know these football megastars were related?

PAUL POGBA

Paul's brother Florentin plays for Saint-Etienne... ...and other brother Mathias plays for Sparta Rotterdam!

YANNICK BOLASIE

The Everton ace is cousins with Brighton winger Kazenga LuaLua, and ex-Newcastle and Blackpool striker Lomana LuaLua!

GONZALO HIGUAIN

The Juventus goal king's brother Federico plays as a forward for Columbus Crew!

ALEX SONG

Song's uncle Rigobert is a Cameroon legend, and used to play for Liverpool!

HERE COMES 2017!

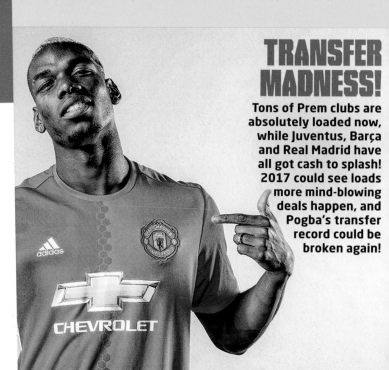

MATCH thinks 2017 will be one of the biggest years in footy history! Here's what you need to look out for...

TRANSFER MADNESS!

Tons of Prem clubs are absolutely loaded now, while Juventus, Barça and Real Madrid have all got cash to splash! 2017 could see loads more mind-blowing deals happen, and Pogba's transfer record could be broken again!

FOOTY'S COMING HOME!

This season's Champions League final is taking place in the UK at Cardiff's Principality Stadium! MATCH can't wait to see over 74,000 fans fill the quality ground, especially if a British team manages to make it all the way!

TOP TOURNAMENTS!

There's no World Cup or European Championship in 2017, but we've still got the Africa Cup Of Nations to look forward to in January and the Confederations Cup in the summer. Sweet!

25 YEARS OF THE PREMIER LEAGUE!

2017 is the 25th anniversary of the first Prem season! Let's hope it celebrates in style with loads of awesome goals, an epic title race and more crazy drama!

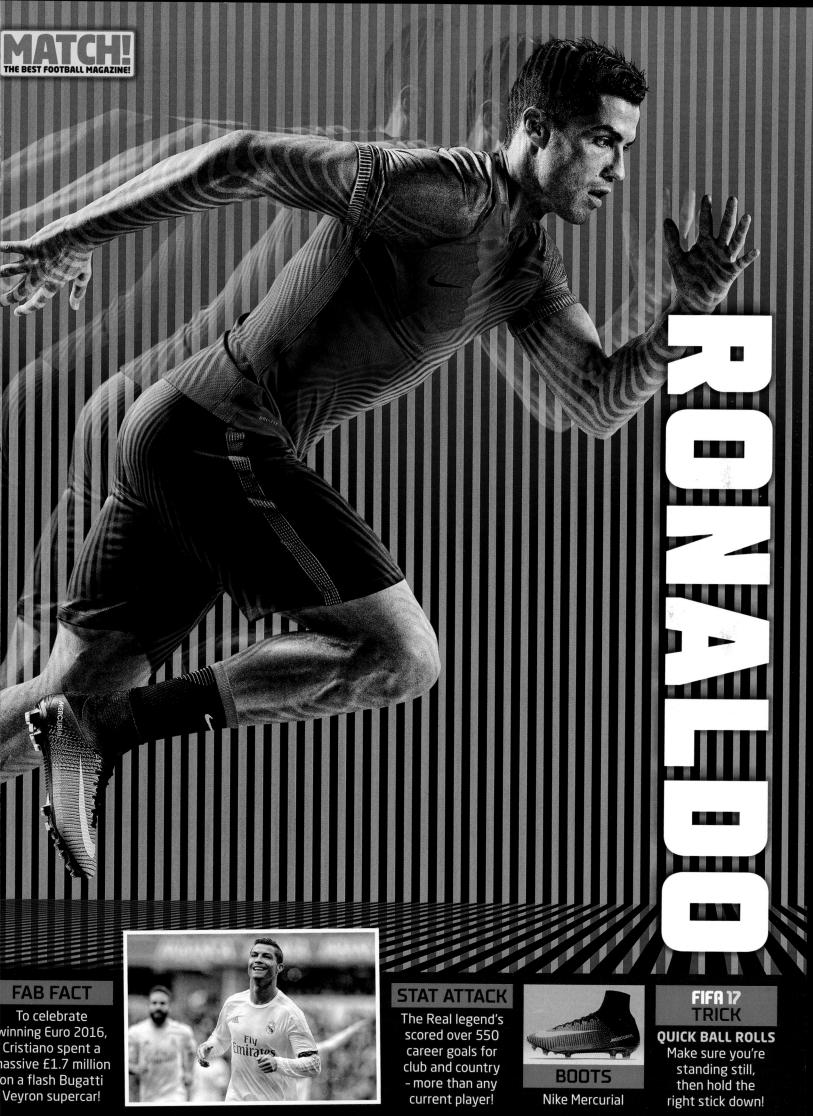

MATCH!
THE BEST FOOTBALL MAGAZINE!

RONALDO

FAB FACT
To celebrate winning Euro 2016, Cristiano spent a massive £1.7 million on a flash Bugatti Veyron supercar!

STAT ATTACK
The Real legend's scored over 550 career goals for club and country - more than any current player!

BOOTS
Nike Mercurial

FIFA 17 TRICK
QUICK BALL ROLLS
Make sure you're standing still, then hold the right stick down!

ULTIMATE GUIDE TO...
MARCUS RASHFORD!

MATCH tells you everything you need to know about one of the hottest wonderkids in the world right now!

LETHAL FINISHING

There aren't many Prem strikers more clinical than Rashford. When he gets a chance, he usually finds the back of the net – his shots-to-goal ratio is top class!

FACT FILE
Age: 18
Club: Man. United
Position: Striker
Boots: Nike Mercurial Superfly

3.2
Last season, Rashford took just over three shots per goal!

RASH REVEALED!
The England & United young gun reveals all about himself!

BEST GOAL
"It was against West Ham last season in the FA Cup. It was right in front of thousands of United fans, too! But the one I enjoyed most was my debut goal against Arsenal."

FAVE SPORTS STAR...
"Cristiano Ronaldo."
...& TOP FOOTY MOMENT
"Definitely making my Man. United debut."

TOUGHEST OPPONENT
"Tottenham and Liverpool were the two best teams I played against last season, but Arsenal's Laurent Koscielny was a really tough opponent."

DEALING WITH THE FAME
"I don't go out as much as I used to. I get recognised a lot now, but I guess that's all part of being a Man. United player."

STRIKER'S INSTINCT

When he's in the penalty area, the United young gun always seems to find himself in the right place at the right time. It's not down to luck - Rash times his runs perfectly and can sense where the ball will land to get on the end of a chance!

BAGS OF PACE

Marcus has the one thing defenders fear most - lightning speed! He uses his rapid pace to run in behind opposition back lines, and he's just as dangerous when running at opponents with the ball!

170
Rashford's first four Man. United goals came in 170 minutes!

TOP TEKKERS

He mainly plays up front now, but Rash played a lot of youth football as a winger or No.10, so he's got loads of tricks and flicks to beat players with. He loves a stepover or a cheeky Cruyff turn!

MARC'S FAVES!

Marcus tells MATCH about his favourite things!

Food
"Chicken and rice made by my mum. I could eat it every day!"

Music
"I listen to R&B and hip hop. I like Drake and Chris Brown."

Fave Film
"Fast & Furious."

Mobile phone
"I've got an iPhone. I couldn't live without it!"

XBOX or PlayStation
"PlayStation."

Best subject at school
"Maths."

NOW TURN OVER FOR MORE RED-HOT WONDERKIDS!

TOP TEENS!

Rashford isn't the only teenage sensation ready to rip up 2017! Check out these young guns from across Europe who are all set for massive years, too!

OUSMANE DEMBELE
Age: 19 ★ Forward
Dortmund ★ France

Dembele was linked with loads of big Euro clubs after bagging 12 goals and five assists in his debut Ligue 1 season for Rennes. He sealed a massive £13 million move to Dortmund last summer, and we can't wait to see the rapid forward tearing up the Bundesliga in 2017!

TOP FIVE SKILLS

Skill	Rating
DRIBBLING	9
PACE	9
FINISHING	8
CREATIVITY	7
MOVEMENT	7

HE'S THE NEXT...
FRANCK RIBERY

GIANLUIGI DONNARUMMA
Age: 17 ★ Goalkeeper
AC Milan ★ Italy

Donnarumma has been compared with Italy ace Gianluigi Buffon ever since he became Serie A's youngest ever goalkeeper in 2015. The AC Milan No.1 is one of the tallest players in the league, and uses his height to dominate his goal. Can he become a footy legend like his hero Buffon?

TOP FIVE SKILLS

Skill	Rating
REACH	9
DIVING	8
ONE-ON-ONE	8
REFLEXES	8
POSITIONING	7

HE'S THE NEXT...
XABI ALONSO

RUBEN NEVES
Age: 19 ★ Midfielder
Porto ★ Portugal

Neves made a huge impact on Portuguese football last season, and he looks set for a massive future with both club and country. He stands out because he plays with so much intelligence and consistency for a teenager and controls games in the middle of the park - that's why he's Porto's youngest ever captain. Quality!

TOP FIVE SKILLS

Skill	Rating
BRAIN	9
PASSING	9
POSITIONING	8
TACKLING	7
VISION	7

RENATO SANCHES
Age: 19 ★ Midfielder
Bayern Munich ★ Portugal

Portugal's youngest player at Euro 2016 was also one of their biggest stars! The 19-year-old was picked as the Young Player Of The Tournament as his country won their first ever major trophy! We reckon the £27.5 million man plays like Man. United star Paul Pogba, bossing games with his box-to-box energy and top-quality passing!

HE'S THE NEXT…
PAUL POGBA

TOP FIVE SKILLS

Skill	Rating
STAMINA	9
DRIBBLING	8
PASSING	8
POWER	8
SHOOTING	7

BREEL EMBOLO
Age: 19 ★ Striker
Schalke ★ Switzerland

Schalke broke their transfer record to sign Embolo for £20 million in 2016 after he scored ten league goals and won his third Swiss title with Basel. The Switzerland ace can run with the ball out wide or from central midfield, but his best position is as a powerhouse centre forward that bullies defenders. He's a beast!

HE'S THE NEXT…
ROMELU LUKAKU

TOP FIVE SKILLS

Skill	Rating
POWER	9
SPEED	9
LINK-UP	8
DRIBBLING	7
FINISHING	7

'S THE NEXT…
IANLUIGI BUFFON

BIG MATCH! QUIZ

PREMIER LEAGUE SPECIAL

KSIOlajidebt

You Tube STAR!

MORE VIDEOS >

Which Premier League star has turned into FIFA YouTube legend KSI in this pic?

Sturridge

MATCH MATHS!

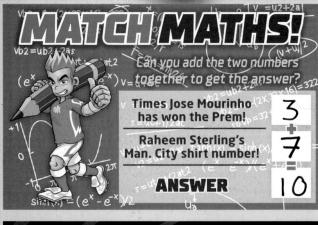

Can you add the two numbers together to get the answer?

Times Jose Mourinho has won the Prem!	3
Raheem Sterling's Man. City shirt number!	+ 7 =
ANSWER	10

FREAKY FACES!

Which Premier League striker has been given a bonkers makeover in this crazy pic?

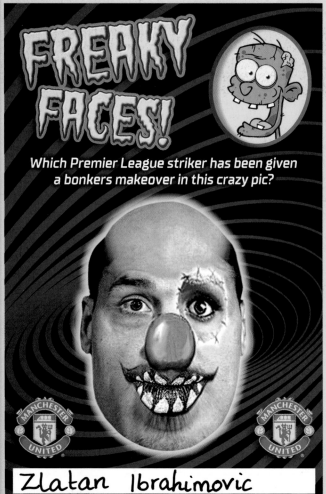

Zlatan Ibrahimovic

THE NICKNAME GAME!

Match these Premier League clubs with their crazy nicknames!

Stoke	Burnley	Everton	Bournemouth
1	2	3	4
A	B	C	D
Toffees	Cherries	Potters	Clarets

GROUNDED!

Which awesome Premier League team play their home games here?

Middlesborough

FOOTY MIS-MATCH

Spot the ten differences between these pics!

1 Emre Can shirt	6 2ND camera
2 Rob Holding's name	7 Footy fan wearing pink
3 Henderson 3 red stripes	8 Alexis left foot missing
4 Xhaka Right boot	9 Mignolet black shoulder
5 Clyne #2 (reversed)	10 Top right no fans

ANSWERS ON PAGE 94

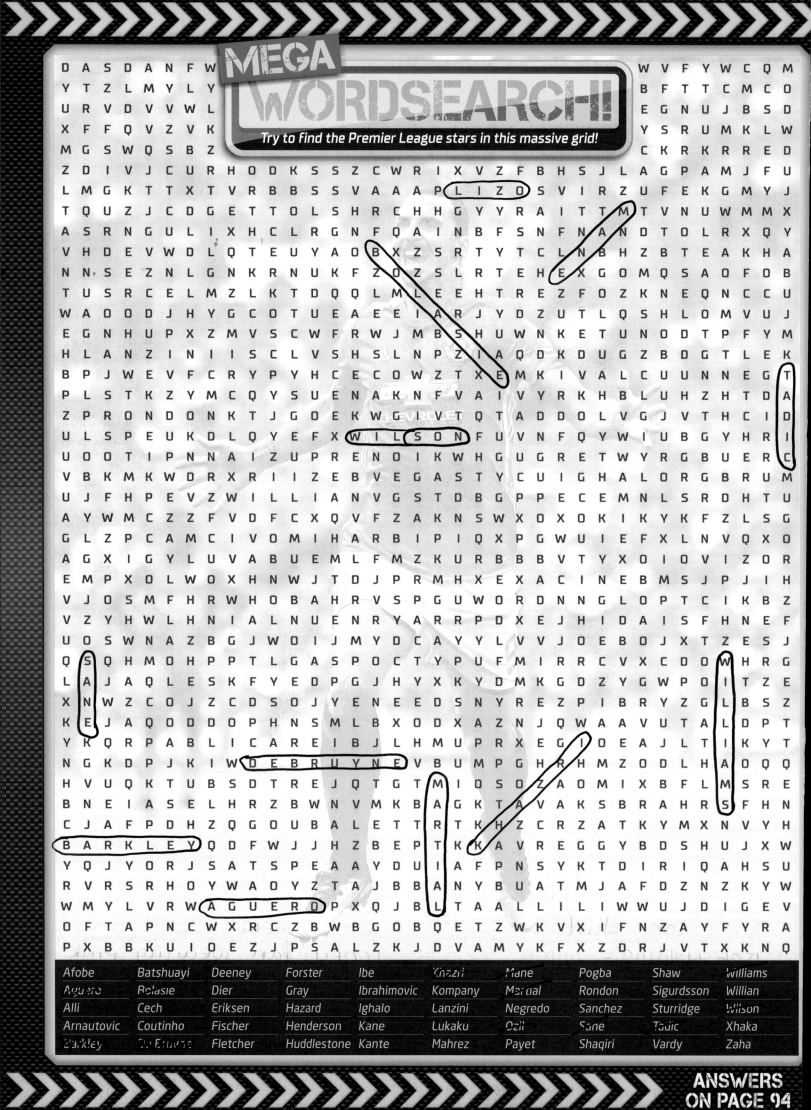

MEGA WORDSEARCH!

Try to find the Premier League stars in this massive grid!

Afobe	Batshuayi	Deeney	Forster	Ibe	Khazri	Mane	Pogba	Shaw	Williams
Aguero	Bolasie	Dier	Gray	Ibrahimovic	Kompany	Martial	Rondon	Sigurdsson	Willian
Alli	Cech	Eriksen	Hazard	Ighalo	Lanzini	Negredo	Sanchez	Sturridge	Wilson
Arnautovic	Coutinho	Fischer	Henderson	Kane	Lukaku	Ozil	Sane	Tadic	Xhaka
Barkley	De Bruyne	Fletcher	Huddlestone	Kante	Mahrez	Payet	Shaqiri	Vardy	Zaha

ANSWERS ON PAGE 94

DE BRUYNE

MATCH!
THE BEST FOOTBALL MAGAZINE!

FAB FACT

KDB became
Man. City's most
xpensive signing
r when he moved
The Etihad for
5 million in 2015!

STAT ATTACK

He equalled the
Bundesliga record
in 2014-15 when he
bagged 20 assists
for Wolfsburg.
His vision rocks!

BOOTS

Nike Mercurial

FIFA 17 TRICK

THE FLICK UP
Flick the
right stick
up three

SNAPPED!
BEST OF 2016! PART ONE

Comfy Franck!

All Ribery needs now is some tea and biscuits!

TWO SUGARS, PLEASE!

Selfie gone wrong!

Nice smile, Riyad, but aren't you forgetting something?

CHEESE... HOLD ON, WHERE'S MY PHONE?

Cheeky Vidal!

The Chile ace is a proper joker!

PULL MY FINGER, MATCH!

Taxi for Westwood!

It's been a bad day for the Villa star!

IT'S TIME TO MAKE A SUB!

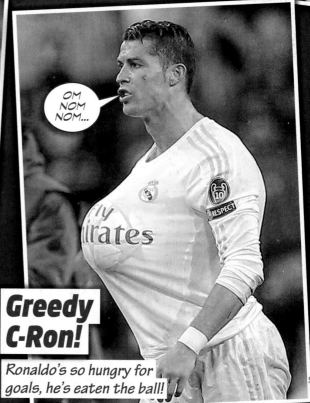

Greedy C-Ron!

Ronaldo's so hungry for goals, he's eaten the ball!

OM NOM NOM...

LIONEL MESSI

ROUTE TO THE THRONE

Messi has been battling Cristiano Ronaldo for the La Liga crown for years, but after winning the last two league titles, there's no doubt who rules in Spain! With over 300 La Liga goals, Leo is Spanish footy's greatest ever player!

2015-16 STATS

Games	33
Goals	26
Assists	16
Mins per goal	105

ROYAL MOMENTS!

KING OF EUROPE

Before the 2009 CL Final, footy experts said Leo was rubbish in the air! He silenced those critics with an awesome header against Man. United to bag the cup for Barça!

SIX OF THE BEST

2009 was defo the greatest year of his career for trophies! Barcelona won a ridiculous six trophies, with Messi scoring 38 goals in all competitions. He bagged his first Ballon d'Or by a record margin, too!

5 BALLONS D'OR

Nobody has been named the world's best player as many times as Messi!

WEAPONS ARMOURY
✓ Creative Genius
✓ Deadly Dribbling
✓ Lethal Finishing

91

In 2012, Messi broke the record for goals scored in a calendar year!

TROPHY CABINET

La Liga:
2004-05, 2005-06, 2008-09, 2009-10, 2010-11, 2012-13, 2014-15, 2015-16

Copa del Rey:
2008-09, 2011-12, 2014-15, 2015-16

Spanish Super Cup:
2005, 2006, 2009, 2010, 2011, 2013, 2016

Champions League:
2005-06, 2008-09, 2010-11, 2014-15

UEFA Super Cup:
2009, 2011, 2015

FIFA Club World Cup:
2009, 2011, 2015

GOALSCORING KING

After winning another Champions League in 2011, Leo went on a red-hot run the following season. In total, he scored 73 times in all comps for the Spanish giants, breaking the world record for goals in one season. Crazy!

TRIO'S TREBLE

In 2014-15, Messi was joined by Luis Suarez and, alongside Neymar, they became the most dangerous front three ever! They won La Liga, the Copa del Rey and CL, hitting 122 goals between them!

STARS' CARS!

Check out the speed machines top footy stars drive!

MEMPHIS

ROLLS ROYCE PHANTOM
Price: £351,000
0-60: 5.6 seconds
Top Speed: 150mph

CLYNE

BENTLEY CONTINENTAL GTC
Price: £144,000
0-60: 4.8 seconds
Top Speed: 188mph

SANCHEZ

LAMBORGHINI AVENTADOR
Price: £260,000
0-60: 2.8 seconds
Top Speed: 217mph

ROONEY

BMW I8
Price: £112,000
0-60: 4.3 seconds
Top Speed: 155mph

POGBA

ALVES

MASERATI GRANTURISMO
Price: £110,000
0-60: 4.4 seconds
Top Speed: 188mph

FERRARI FF
Price: £227,000
0-60: 3.7 seconds
Top Speed: 208mph

DE BRUYNE

MERCEDES G 63 AMG
Price: £123,000
0-60: 5.3 seconds
Top Speed: 130mph

BMW X6
Price: £78,000
0-60: 4.2 seconds
Top Speed: 155mph

HAZARD

PORSCHE 918 SPYDER

Price: £661,000

0-60: 2.7 seconds

Top Speed: 211mph

IBRAHIMOVIC

PORSCHE 911 TURBO

Price: £120,000

0-60: 3.1 seconds

Top Speed: 197mph

TOURE

911 HUL

BLIND

CHEVROLET CORVETTE STINGRAY

Price: £40,000

0-60: 3.8 seconds

Top Speed: 195mph

GG C 7111

ASTON MARTIN VANQUISH

Price: £212,000

0-60: 3.6 seconds

Top Speed: 201mph

FABREGAS

WORKS

FERRARI 458 SPIDER

Price: £200,000

0-60: 3.3 seconds

Top Speed: 199mph

NEYMAR

BENZEMA

BUGATTI VEYRON 450 LA FINALE

Price: £1.2 million

0-60: 2.5 seconds

Top Speed: 267mph

PAGANI HUAYRA

Price: £1.77 million

0-60: 2.8 seconds

Top Speed: 238mph

RONALDO

HE SAID WHAT?

MATCH checks out the craziest footy quotes we've heard in 2016!

"I THOUGHT THEY'D WON THE EUROS THE WAY THEY CELEBRATED AT THE END. IT WAS UNBELIEVABLE."

Cristiano Ronaldo talks after Portugal's 1-1 draw with Iceland at Euro 2016. He's not bitter of course... that's not his style!

"IT HAPPENED WHILE DRIVING AND THE PHONE WAS IN MY POCKET."

Joleon Lescott explains how he managed to tweet a photo of a sports car after Aston Villa's 6-0 home defeat by Liverpool. LOL!

"I REALLY LOVE THIS SONG. I WOULD LIKE TO SAY OUR DEFENCE IS TERRIFIED, BUT I CAN'T AGREE."

Mats Hummels chats about the Will Grigg song before Germany took on Northern Ireland at Euro 2016.

"NO MATTER WHO WE'RE PLAYING, WE PLAY THREE IN MIDFIELD – DRINKWATER IN THE MIDDLE AND KANTE EITHER SIDE."

Ex-Leicester chief scout Steve Walsh on why The Foxes' midfield was so good last season!

"HEY MAN, WE ARE IN CHAMPIONS LEAGUE. DILLY DING, DILLY DONG. COME ON. YOU SPEAK ABOUT BLAH, BLAH, BLAH BUT WE ARE IN CHAMPIONS LEAGUE. COME ON MAN, FANTASTIC!"

Claudio Ranieri's famous reaction to Champions League qualification has gone down in Leicester history.

"USUALLY I HAVE A SECOND PAIR, BUT UNTIL NOW I COULD NOT FIND THEM BECAUSE IT'S REALLY DIFFICULT LOOKING FOR GLASSES WITHOUT GLASSES!"

Jurgen Klopp speaks after Liverpool's last-gasp 5-4 victory over Norwich last season. He lost his glasses in the celebrations and couldn't find his replacement pair!

MATCH!
THE BEST FOOTBALL MAGAZINE!

ALLI

FAB FACT
The Tottenham
ar is the youngest
dfielder ever to hit
double figures in
Premier League
season. Hero!

STAT ATTACK
Alli got nine
Premier League
assists in 2015-16
– and seven were
for team-mate
Harry Kanel

BOOTS
Adidas ACS 16

FIFA 17
TRICK
THE ROULETTE
Push the right stick
down, then rotate
270 degrees

IF FOOTY STARS WERE... EMOJIS!

Whether it's a wink or an alien head, we love seeing footy megastars pulling funny faces like Emojis. Check them out!

PIZZA PRAY

MR. ANGRY

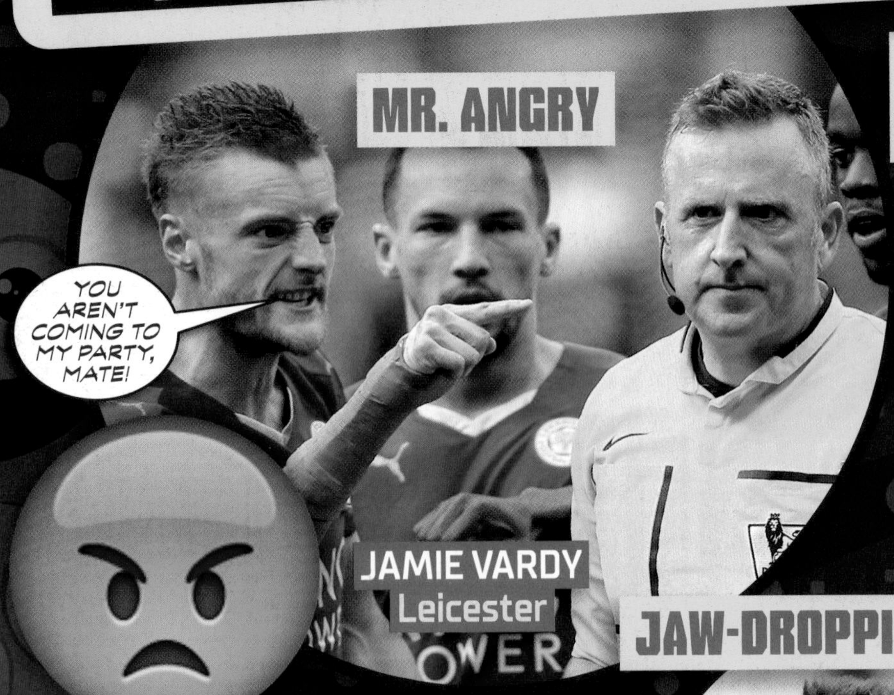

JAMIE VARDY
Leicester

SILLY SANCHEZ

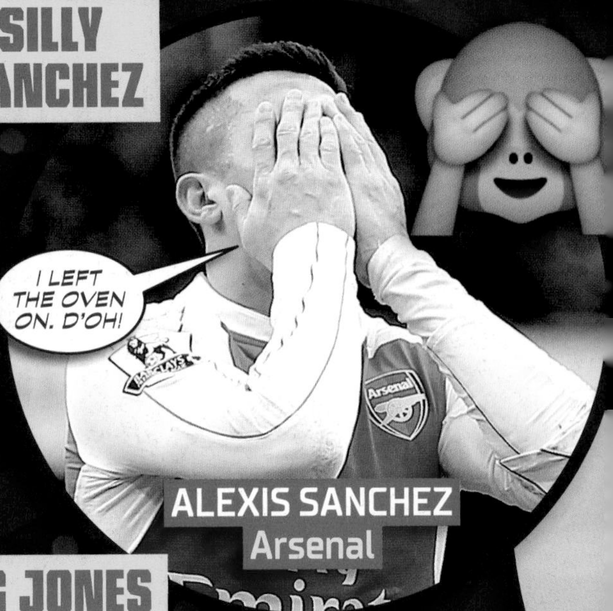

ALEXIS SANCHEZ
Arsenal

JAW-DROPPING JONES

PHIL JONES
Man. United

MARCO THE MONKEY

MARCO REUS
Dortmund

SKIPPER SMOOCH

WES MORGAN
Leicester

CHEEKY JOSE

CLAUDIO RANIERI
Leicester

THERE'S SOMETHING IN MY EYE!

JOSE MOURINHO
Man. United

WHO WANTS TO JOIN MY BAND?

ROCKSTAR RED
JAMES MILNER
Liverpool

CRY-BABY CRISTIANO

DIEGO'S DENTIST CHECK

ARE MY TEETH CLEAN?

DIEGO COSTA
Chelsea

NAUGHTY NEYMAR

THIS IS MY DOG IMPRESSION!

NEYMAR
Barcelona

SOMEONE STOLE MY MIRROR!

CRISTIANO RONALDO
Real Madrid

BANDAGE FAIL

WHERE AM I?

VEDRAN CORLUKA
Lokomotiv Moscow

LOL-ERPOOL

MESUT THE MARTIAN

SHADY SAM

I'M THE COOLEST ENGLAND GAFFER EVER!

SAM ALLARDYCE
England

NOT FUNNY, GUYS!

MESUT OZIL
Arsenal

YOU'RE HILARIOUS, MATCH!

DANIEL STURRIDGE
Liverpool

MATCH! 31

BIG MATCH! QUIZ

FOOTBALL LEAGUE SPECIAL

jobswap

Which League 1 goal machine has become a lumberjack?

Scott Golbourne

Richard Stearman

Karl Henry

Christophe Berra

CLUB SHARERS!

★ ★ ★ ★ ★ ★ ★

Which Championship club have these heroes all played for?

Tomasz Kuszczak

Sam Winnall

BACK TO THE FUTURE

Name the League 2 legend who's gone back in time to become a Roman Gladiator!

FLIPPED!

Name the Championship superstar who's had his face messed up in this weird pic!

CAMERA SHY!

Can you name the quality Football League players hiding in these pics?

5 QUESTIONS ON... SHEFFIELD WEDNESDAY

1. Which famous stadium do The Owls play their home matches at?

2. True or False? The 2015-16 play-off finalists are the oldest team in the Football League!

3. What awesome country does rock-solid shot-stopper Keiren Westwood play for?

4. Which side did Wednesday beat in the play-off semi-finals last season – Brighton, Derby, Bristol City or Huddersfield?

5. How old is their tough-tackling centre-back Sam Hutchinson – 24, 25, 26 or 27 years old?

GUESS THE WINNERS!

2016

2015

Which teams won League 1 in these seasons?

2014

2013

SPOT THE SPONSOR!

Name the Football League teams with these sponsors on their shirts!

1.

2.

3.

4.

5.

6.

MATCH! WINNER!

Who scored the opening goal of the 2016-17 season for Fulham against Newcastle?

ANSWERS ON PAGE 94

CROSSWORD CRUNCH!

Use these clues to fill in MATCH's Football League crossword!

ACROSS

7. Quality Brighton winger, Anthony _ _ _ _ _ _ _ _ _! (9)

8. Lethal Scotland and Norwich goal machine! (6,8)

11. Essex-based team that plays in League 2! (10)

15. Total number of teams in League 1 and 2 combined! (5,5)

16. Nickname of Cardiff, The _ _ _ _ _ _ _ _ _! (9)

18. Leyton Orient signed ace midfielder Liam Kelly from this League 1 team! (6)

21. Name of Bury's stadium! (4,4)

22. Sports brand who designed Southend's kit this season and make the Magista boot! (4)

23. Newcastle signed Matt Ritchie from this Prem club! (11)

24. Last season's Championship play-off final winners! (4)

25. Bradford, Swindon, MK Dons, Coventry and Chesterfield all play in this epic league! (6,3)

DOWN

1. Shirt number of deadly Carlisle goal grabber Jabo Ibehre! (8)

2. First name shared by Fulham's Parker and Derby's Carson! (5)

3. Number of clubs in League 1 that start with the letter 'C'! (5)

4. The League 2 champions in the 2015-16 season! (11)

5. Reading boss Jaap Stam used to play for this Prem club! (10,6)

6. Walsall and Philippines keeper, _ _ _ _ _ _ _ _ _ _ _ _ _ _! (4,9)

9. Class League 2 team who are known as The Mariners! (7)

10. Scotland goalkeeper who left Cardiff last summer! (5,8)

12. Colour of Portsmouth, Ipswich, Peterborough and Wimbledon's home shirts! (4)

13. Awesome League 1 London club _ _ _ _ _ _ _ _ _! (9)

14. Wigan and Northern Ireland goal king, _ _ _ _ _ _ _ _ _! (4,5)

17. Glanford Park is home to this wicked League 2 team! (10)

19. Club who lost last season's League 1 play-off final! (8)

20. Championship club who are nicknamed The Bees! (9)

ANSWERS ON PAGE 94

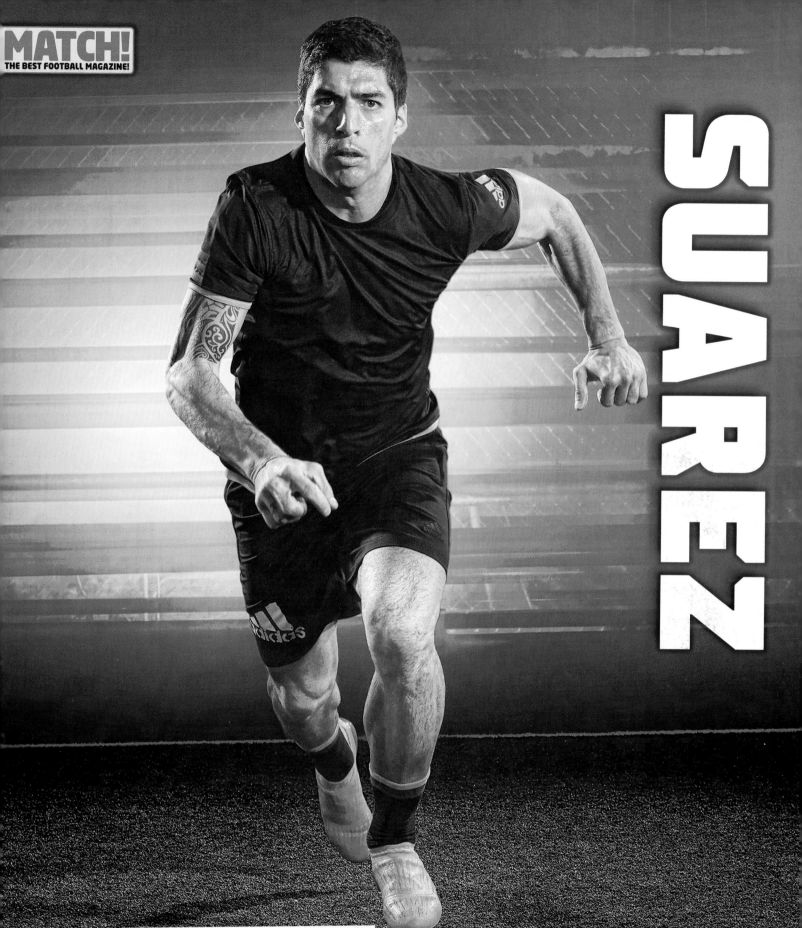

SUAREZ

FAB FACT

Suarez is the first
player to score more
La Liga goals in a
single season than
Ronaldo and Messi
since 2008-09!

STAT ATTACK

All 40 of the
deadly striker's
league goals in
2015-16 came
from inside the
penalty area!

BOOTS

Adidas X 16.1

FIFA 17
TRICK

STOP AND TURN
Flick the right stick
up and then to either
side in the direction
you want to

PIERRE-EMERICK AUBAMEYANG

BVB 09

ROUTE TO THE THRONE

Even though Bayern boss the Bundesliga, nobody dominates defences like Aubameyang! The Dortmund hero can charge through any back line with his frightening pace, and when he gets a chance, he very rarely misses!

WEAPONS ARMOURY
- ✓ Crazy Speed
- ✓ Lethal Finishing
- ✓ Epic Movement

ROYAL MOMENTS!

BREAKOUT SEASON

In 2012-13, Aubameyang established himself as one of Europe's top talents! He bagged 19 goals and nine assists for Saint-Etienne in Ligue 1, which earned him a move to Dortmund!

RECORD BREAKER

PEA made an electric start to the 2015-16 season – he scored in his first eight league games! Nobody in Bundesliga history had scored in more than the first six matches before!

2015-16 STATS

Games	31
Goals	25
Assists	5
Shots per goal	4.72

3.7 SECONDS

Aubameyang once ran 30 metres in less than four seconds. Crazy!

0.55

In his last five seasons, Auba's strike rate is better than a goal every two games!

TROPHY CABINET

French League Cup:
2012-13
German Super Cup:
2013, 2014

KING OF AFRICA

The speed king's incredible form at the start of last season helped him seal the 2015 African Footballer Of The Year Award, becoming the first Gabonese player to do so. Total legend!

BUNDESLIGA BOSS

The Dortmund star finished 2015-16 with 39 goals in all competitions, and was named the Bundesliga Player Of The Year ahead of Bayern Munich stars Robert Lewandowski and Manuel Neuer. Hero!

WIN!
iPOD TOUCH
SEE PAGE
52!

ULTIMATE PLAYER!

MATCH picks the best players in the world to help create the planet's ultimate footy star – then we want you to have your say for the chance to win an awesome Apple iPod Touch!

VISION

MY PICK ✓

DAVID SILVA
MIDFIELDER ★ MAN. CITY

Silva is one player we can't get enough of watching! He spots runs before the strikers have even moved and executes the final pass to perfection. Ledge!

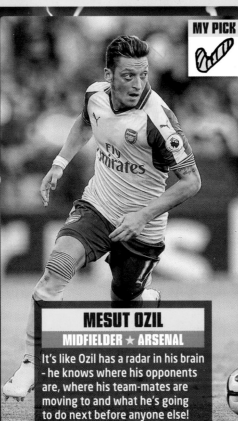

MY PICK

MESUT OZIL
MIDFIELDER ★ ARSENAL

It's like Ozil has a radar in his brain - he knows where his opponents are, where his team-mates are moving to and what he's going to do next before anyone else!

MY PICK ✓

ANDRES INIESTA
MIDFIELDER ★ BARCELONA

Spain legend Iniesta plays footy like he's got eyes in the back of his head! He gets on the ball and plays passes that only a few players in the world can see!

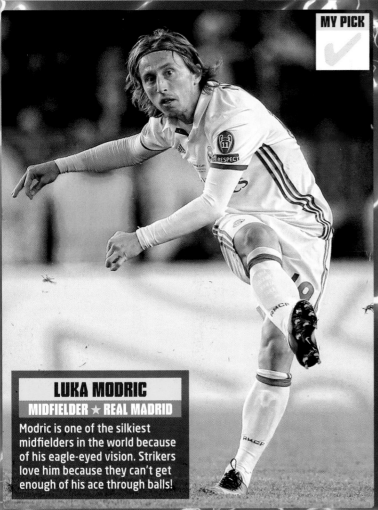

MY PICK ✓

LUKA MODRIC
MIDFIELDER ★ REAL MADRID

Modric is one of the silkiest midfielders in the world because of his eagle-eyed vision. Strikers love him because they can't get enough of his ace through balls!

MY PICK ✓

LIONEL MESSI
FORWARD ★ BARCELONA

Messi has it all as a footballer, but none of it would be possible without his mind-blowing vision! It helps him stay one step ahead of his opponents all the time!

HEADING

MY PICK

SERGIO RAMOS
CENTRE-BACK ★ REAL MADRID

Ramos' attacking headers are just as good as his defensive headers. He's a rock at the back, and one of Real's biggest threats when they win set-pieces!

MY PICK

ARITZ ADURIZ
STRIKER ★ ATHLETIC BILBAO

Aduriz is getting on a bit, but he's still got one of the best headers in the world. Bilbao's players know that if they whip in a decent cross, Aduriz will head it in!

MY PICK

DIEGO GODIN
CENTRE-BACK ★ ATLETICO

Godin dominates strikers with his aerial ability and he's scored in a World Cup, Champo League final and La Liga title-winning match - all with his head. What a hero!

MY PICK

CRISTIANO RONALDO
FORWARD ★ REAL MADRID

Ron's a footy legend, and one of his most underrated skills is his heading. When he jumps it's like he's got springs in his boots, plus he hangs in the air for ages!

MY PICK

ANDY CARROLL
STRIKER ★ WEST HAM

Carroll is the No.1 Prem aerial king and is unplayable when he's on top of his game. He's a giant, and nobody can out-jump him when he times his leaps right!

FREE-KICKS

MATCH loves dead-ball demons – and these guys are masters!

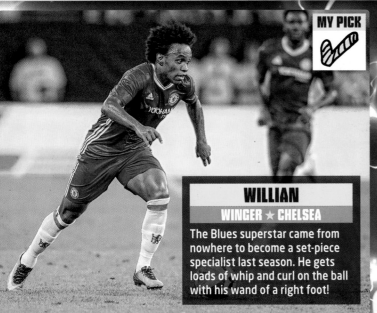

MY PICK

WILLIAN
WINGER ★ CHELSEA

The Blues superstar came from nowhere to become a set-piece specialist last season. He gets loads of whip and curl on the ball with his wand of a right foot!

MY PICK

HAKAN CALHANOGLU
MIDFIELDER ★ B. LEVERKUSEN

Calhanoglu's the best FK taker on FIFA, and it's easy to see why when you watch him in real life. It's like giving away a penalty when Hakan's on set-pieces!

MY PICK

DIMITRI PAYET
MIDFIELDER ★ WEST HAM

Payet proved last season that he's one of the best FK takers on the planet. He always finds the top corners and leaves keepers guessing which side he'll go!

MY PICK

CHRISTIAN ERIKSEN
MIDFIELDER ★ TOTTENHAM

Eriksen is a free-kick master! He's Spurs' No.1 set-piece taker, and is just as good at setting up goals from dead balls as he is scoring directly from them!

MY PICK

GARETH BALE
WINGER ★ REAL MADRID

Bale's free-kick technique is just like Ronaldo's, but his accuracy is miles better than his team-mate! He proved that at Euro 2016 with some proper worldies!

POWER

MY PICK ✓

ROBERT HUTH
CENTRE-BACK ★ LEICESTER

Huth's like a brick wall standing between opponents and The Foxes' goal! The man mountain bullies strikers with his monster power and massive frame!

MY PICK ✓

PAUL POGBA
MIDFIELDER ★ MAN. UNITED

Pog uses his explosive running style - with aggression, power and pace - to boss games from midfield. When he runs from box to box, he's like a steam train!

MY PICK ✓

ADEBAYO AKINFENWA
STRIKER ★ WYCOMBE

No CB in the world can outmuscle Wycombe ace Akinfenwa! When he holds the ball up, there's no chance of getting it - opponents just bounce off him. Beast mode!

MY PICK ✓

ROMELU LUKAKU
STRIKER ★ EVERTON

Big Belgium bruiser Lukaku loves barging defenders out of the way before ripping nets. His massive power scares opponents just as much as his deadly left foot!

MY PICK

ZLATAN IBRAHIMOVIC
STRIKER ★ MAN. UNITED

Zlatan is a total footy legend, and one of his biggest attributes is his unbelievable strength. He uses that power to hit thunderous shots with his rocket right foot!

TRICKS

MY PICK ✓

CRISTIANO RONALDO
FORWARD ★ REAL MADRID
Ronaldo is definitely one of the flashest footy stars around, and he's famous for leaving defenders on their backsides after busting out loads of sick stepovers!

MY PICK ✓

DOUGLAS COSTA
WINGER ★ BAYERN MUNICH
Douglas Costa is the Bundesliga's No.1 skiller! The Samba superstar absolutely ruins players with incredible foot speed, epic feints and ridiculous rainbow flicks!

MY PICK ✓

RIYAD MAHREZ
WINGER ★ LEICESTER
Mahrez uses his quick feet to constantly make defenders look silly! He loves a nutmeg, and his elastico against Stoke last season was totally mind-blowing!

MY PICK ✓

NEYMAR
FORWARD ★ BARCELONA
Neymar can bust out tricks in his sleep - stepovers, flip-flaps, rabonas, roulette spins, Cruyff turns - the Brazil legend has them all! He's a total skills magician!

MY PICK ✓

YANNICK BOLASIE
WINGER ★ EVERTON
Bolasie loves busting out wicked tricks when he's running at full pace! Defenders just can't handle his mind-boggling combo of rapid dribbling speed and silky skills!

WORK-RATE

The batteries on these crazy lung-busters never run out !

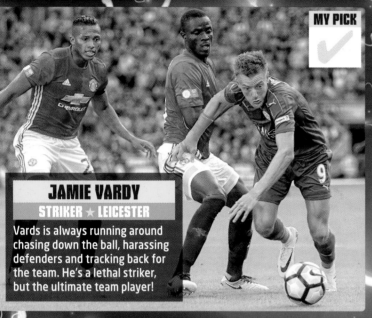

MY PICK ✓

JAMIE VARDY
STRIKER ★ LEICESTER

Vards is always running around chasing down the ball, harassing defenders and tracking back for the team. He's a lethal striker, but the ultimate team player!

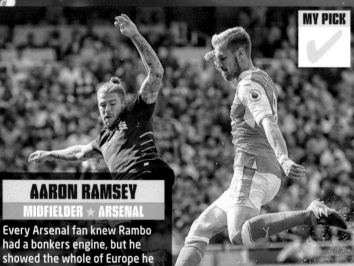

MY PICK ✓

AARON RAMSEY
MIDFIELDER ★ ARSENAL

Every Arsenal fan knew Rambo had a bonkers engine, but he showed the whole of Europe he could run forever when he ripped up Euro 2016 with Wales. Hero!

MY PICK ✓

JAMES MILNER
MIDFIELDER ★ LIVERPOOL

The consistent Milner always works his socks off and you know what you're going to get from him every game. The Reds midfielder never stops running!

MY PICK ✓

LUIS SUAREZ
STRIKER ★ BARCELONA

Suarez is one of those rare breeds - a world-class footballer and goalscorer who also works as hard as anyone else on the planet. His passion is off the charts!

MY PICK ✓

N'GOLO KANTE
MIDFIELDER ★ CHELSEA

The Blues new boy covers so much ground - it's like he does the work of two players all by himself! He was a big reason behind Leicester's shock Prem title win last season!

FINISHING

When it comes to net-busting, these heroes do it in their sleep!

MY PICK ✓

CRISTIANO RONALDO
FORWARD ★ REAL MADRID

When C-Ron gets on the ball, he only ever has one thing on his mind - to rip net! That's why he's scored more career goals than any other star currently playing!

MY PICK

LUIS SUAREZ
STRIKER ★ BARCELONA

Suarez scored a mind-boggling 59 goals in all competitions last season - way more than Messi and Neymar! He also won the La Liga Golden Boot with 40 goals!

MY PICK ✓

SERGIO AGUERO
STRIKER ★ MAN. CITY

Aguero's ice-cool in front of goal, and catches keepers out with early shots before they can get themselves set. He's one of the deadliest strikers in Prem history!

MY PICK ✓

LIONEL MESSI
FORWARD ★ BARCELONA

One-on-ones, finesse finishes, long-range rockets, sick volleys - Leo does it all! But he's most famous for his cheeky left-foot dinked shots over the keeper!

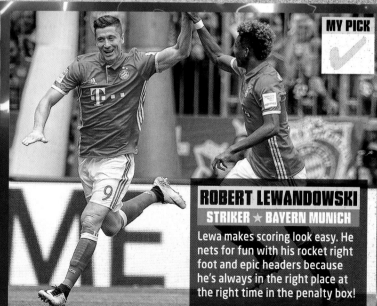

MY PICK ✓

ROBERT LEWANDOWSKI
STRIKER ★ BAYERN MUNICH

Lewa makes scoring look easy. He nets for fun with his rocket right foot and epic headers because he's always in the right place at the right time in the penalty box!

HANDS

MY PICK ✓

THIBAUT COURTOIS
GOALKEEPER ★ CHELSEA

Courtois has the biggest reach of any GK around. His giant frame means he can stretch his hands out to save any shot - even when it's heading for the top corner!

MY PICK ✓

DAVID DE GEA
GOALKEEPER ★ MAN. UNITED

We reckon De Gea is probably the best shot-stopper on the planet. When it looks easier for a striker to score, somehow the Spain ace pulls off an amazing wondersave!

MY PICK ✓

GIANLUIGI BUFFON
GOALKEEPER ★ JUVENTUS

Buffon's been around for years, but he's as good as ever! His reactions are still mega sharp, and his experience helps him come out on top in one-on-ones!

MY PICK ✓

HUGO LLORIS
GOALKEEPER ★ TOTTENHAM

Lloris is so cool, and he uses that calmness to get the better of strikers when they go through on goal. His shot-stopping and handling rarely let him down!

MY PICK

MANUEL NEUER
GOALKEEPER ★ B. MUNICH

The Bayern legend doesn't get beaten often, hardly ever drops a cross and has lightning reflexes! The ball just sticks to his gloves when he stretches out his hands!

BRAIN

MY PICK ✔

THOMAS MULLER
FORWARD ★ BAYERN MUNICH

The Germany goal king doesn't need rapid speed or monster strength to beat defenders - his class brain does that for him. He's a master at sniffing out goals!

MY PICK ✔

WAYNE ROONEY
FORWARD ★ MAN. UNITED

Rooney's footy brain means he can play as a striker or in midfield and still run games. It also helps him pick out long passes most players can only dream of!

MY PICK ✔

LIONEL MESSI
FORWARD ★ BARCELONA

Footy experts always argue who's better between Messi and Ron, but one skill we reckon Leo defo comes out on top is his mega-quick brain. He's a freak!

MY PICK ✔

ANDRES INIESTA
MIDFIELDER ★ BARCELONA

The Barça playmaker's mega intelligent footy brain has helped him dominate midfields for years. The silky Spaniard is always one step ahead of his marker!

MY PICK ✔

PHILIPP LAHM
FULL-BACK ★ BAYERN MUNICH

Lahm doesn't grab the headlines like his Bayern team-mates, but he's the brains behind it all! He's so clever, he can play as a DM and totally dominate games too!

TACKLING

Some say the art of tackling has gone, but not for these defenders!

MY PICK ✓

VINCENT KOMPANY
CENTRE-BACK ★ MAN. CITY

When City's skipper isn't injured, he's busy bossing strikers! He combines pace, positioning, top tackling and an epic brain to make winning the ball look easy!

MY PICK ✓

JEROME BOATENG
CENTRE-BACK ★ B. MUNICH

Boateng's a classy defender and Bayern and Germany's No.1 CB right now. Whether it's a standing tackle or late sliding challenge, Boateng usually wins the ball!

MY PICK ✓

THIAGO SILVA
CENTRE-BACK ★ PSG

Silva is a tackling expert - you hardly ever see him sliding in and missing the ball or fouling a player. His ace positional skills help him win the ball back cleanly, too!

MY PICK ✓

GIORGIO CHIELLINI
CENTRE-BACK ★ JUVENTUS

The Juve rock is a real out-and-out defender - he uses tough tackles and raw power to make sure he takes everything when he goes to win the ball. Strikers hate him!

MY PICK ✓

LAURENT KOSCIELNY
CENTRE-BACK ★ ARSENAL

Koscielny's a master at winning the ball ahead of strikers. He uses anticipation, pace and top tackling skills to nip in front of opponents and intercept the ball!

SPEED

Sprinting legend Usain Bolt would struggle to keep up with this lot!

MY PICK ✔

GARETH BALE
WINGER ★ REAL MADRID

Not many stars can keep up with Bale when he gets going! His raw power and rapid sprints make him one of the most dangerous attackers on the planet!

MY PICK ✔

THEO WALCOTT
WINGER ★ ARSENAL

Theo's almost uncatchable when he's in full flight! His electric acceleration leaves opponents choking on dust, and he burns away once he hits top gear!

MY PICK ✔

PIERRE-EMERICK AUBAMEYANG
STRIKER ★ B. DORTMUND

Rapid Dortmund speed machine Aubameyang can run the 100m quicker than you can say his name! He totally skins defenders when he bursts past them!

MY PICK ✔

HECTOR BELLERIN
FULL-BACK ★ ARSENAL

Bellerin's electric - he even beat Walcott's record as The Gunners' fastest player in training a few years ago. He's always bombing up and down the right wing!

MY PICK ✔

JAMIE VARDY
STRIKER ★ LEICESTER

Vardy banged home 24 Premier League goals last season, and most of that was down to his pace chasing long balls and destroying teams on the counter-attack!

DRIBBLING

You can't win the ball off these wizards once they get on the ball!

MY PICK ✓

NEYMAR
FORWARD ★ BARCELONA

No wonder Barça score so many goals - they've got Messi on one side and Neymar on the other running defences ragged with their demon dribbling skills!

MY PICK ✓

CRISTIANO RONALDO
FORWARD ★ REAL MADRID

Pace, power, tricks and direct running make Cristiano a beast when he's dribbling. It's one of the reasons he creates so many goalscoring chances for himself!

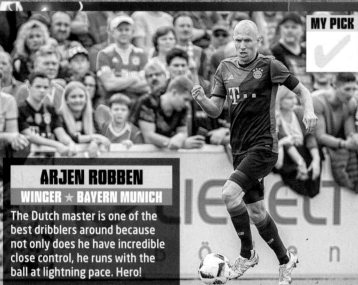

MY PICK ✓

ARJEN ROBBEN
WINGER ★ BAYERN MUNICH

The Dutch master is one of the best dribblers around because not only does he have incredible close control, he runs with the ball at lightning pace. Hero!

MY PICK ✓

LIONEL MESSI
FORWARD ★ BARCELONA

Leo is the king of dribbling! The twinkle-toed Barça legend ties defenders in knots with his close control, quick swivel turns and drops of the shoulder. See ya!

MY PICK ✓

EDEN HAZARD
WINGER ★ CHELSEA

Eden destroys defenders with quick acceleration bursts, direct running and mega-rapid feet! MATCH reckons he's probably the best dribbler in the Prem!

PASSING

MY PICK ✓

SANTI CAZORLA
MIDFIELDER ★ ARSENAL

Classy Gunners playmaker Cazorla often averages more passes per game than anyone in the Prem, and they usually find their target like heat-seeking missiles!

MY PICK ✓

TONI KROOS
MIDFIELDER ★ REAL MADRID

Kroos has some proper big-time team-mates at Real, but he's the top dog when it comes to picking a pass. He's awesome at both long and short balls. Legend!

MY PICK ✓

MARCO VERRATTI
MIDFIELDER ★ PSG

Italy had a pass master bossing their midfield for years in Andrea Pirlo, and Verratti's ready to take over from him. His passing ability is from another universe!

MY PICK ✓

XABI ALONSO
MIDFIELDER ★ B. MUNICH

Alonso starts attacks from deep with his clever passing, while his long passes and killer through balls absolutely shred defences. He's a complete passing machine!

MY PICK ✓

CESC FABREGAS
MIDFIELDER ★ CHELSEA

Cesc opens up defences with his killer passing and laser-guided through balls. Teams just can't afford to let him get his head up when he's near the penalty box!

BUILD YOUR ULTIMATE PLAYER

HEADING
MATCH PICKS:
ANDY CARROLL
YOU PICK:
Carrol

VISION
MATCH PICKS:
MESUT OZIL
YOU PICK:
Ozil

POWER
MATCH PICKS:
ADEBAYO AKINFENWA
YOU PICK:
Pogba

FREE-KICKS
MATCH PICKS:
DIMITRI PAYET
YOU PICK:
Messi

TRICKS
MATCH PICKS:
NEYMAR
YOU PICK:
Neymar

FINISHING
MATCH PICKS:
LIONEL MESSI
YOU PICK:
Suarez

BRAIN
MATCH PICKS:
ANDRES INIESTA
YOU PICK:
Coutinho

WORK-RATE
MATCH PICKS:
N'GOLO KANTE
YOU PICK:
Kante

HANDS
MATCH PICKS:
DAVID DE GEA
YOU PICK:
Neuer

SPEED
MATCH PICKS:
PIERRE-E. AUBAMEYANG
YOU PICK:
Bellerin

TACKLING
MATCH PICKS:
JEROME BOATENG
YOU PICK:
T. Silva

DRIBBLING
MATCH PICKS:
LIONEL MESSI
YOU PICK:
Messi

PASSING
MATCH PICKS:
TONI KROOS
YOU PICK:
Iniesta

WIN!
IPOD TOUCH!

Now pick your Ultimate Player! Just write your players' names into the spaces above, fill out your details below, photocopy this page and send it to MATCH. Then, one lucky winner will be picked at random!

Send to: MATCH Annual 2017, Ultimate Player Competition, MATCH Magazine, Media House, Peterborough, PE2 6EA.

16GB only. Colours include Silver, Blue, Red, Pink, Space Grey and Gold. Closing date: Jan. 31, 2017.

NAME: Druan Shah
DATE OF BIRTH: 21/03/2005
ADDRESS: W4 5EH London
Fairlawn Grove
MOBILE: 0956677808
EMAIL: druanshah@icloud.com

MATCH!
THE BEST FOOTBALL MAGAZINE!

OZIL

FAB FACT
zil's £42.5 million
nove to Arsenal
makes him the
most expensive
German player
of all time!

STAT ATTACK
Ozil created 19
goals in the Prem
last season - more
than any other
player in Europe's
top five leagues!

BOOTS
Adidas ACE 16+

FIFA 17 TRICK
THE BALL HOP
Stand still,
then push the
right stick down
like a button!

DRAW YOUR FOOTY HERO!

Calling all budding artists! MATCH wants you to sketch your fave footy star, on or off the pitch, and send it to us! The best one wins a Prem shirt of their choice!

WIN!

Just photocopy this page,
draw your pic and send it to:
MATCH Annual 2017 - Draw Your
Footy Hero, MATCH Magazine,
Media House, Lynch Wood,
Peterborough, PE2 6EA.
Then we'll pick our fave
picture and send the winner
a footy shirt of their choice!
Closing date: Jan. 31, 2017.

Name:

Date of birth:

Address:

Mobile:

Email:

SERGIO AGUERO

2015-16 STATS

Games	30
Goals	24
Shots per goal	4.96
Mins per goal	99

ROUTE TO THE THRONE

Since Kun joined the Prem back in 2011, no player has scored more goals than the lethal net-buster! It's not just about how many goals he scores, either – Aguero manages to produce match-winning moments when it really matters!

108

In his first five Prem seasons, Aguero averaged a goal every 108 minutes!

1

Sergio is City's all-time top scorer in both Premier League and European football!

ROYAL MOMENTS!

EUROPA LEAGUE HERO

Kun hit 74 goals in 175 La Liga games for Atletico, but his best moment for them came in the 2010 Europa League Final. He got two assists as Atleti beat Fulham 2-1 to lift their first European trophy for 48 years!

FINAL DAY DRAMA

Aguero bagged 23 goals in his debut Prem season, but his incredible injury-time winner against QPR is what everybody remembers most about 2011-12! It's one of the Prem's best ever moments!

WEAPONS ARMOURY

✓ Brilliant Balance
✓ Dangerous Dribbling
✓ Quick Shooting

TROPHY CABINET

Europa League:
2009-10
Intertoto Cup:
2007
UEFA Super Cup:
2010
Premier League:
2011-12, 2013-14
League Cup:
2013-14, 2015-16
Community Shield:
2012

TITLE NUMBER TWO

Two years later, the hitman was celebrating another Prem title at The Etihad. He only played 23 games, but the City star averaged a goal every 90 minutes - scoring 17 times in total. He won his first League Cup winners' medal, too!

GOLDEN BOOT BOSS

Despite scoring tons of goals for City, Kun still hadn't won the Prem Golden Boot after three seasons at the club! That changed in 2014-15 as he thumped home 26 league goals, beating Harry Kane!

BIG MATCH! QUIZ

CHAMPIONS LEAGUE SPECIAL

SWITCH!

Which Champions League striker has changed careers to become a Formula 1 driver?

Auba

5 QUESTIONS ON...

THE CHAMPO LEAGUE

1 Which three footy legends jointly won the Champions League top goalscorer award back in 2014-15?

2 Real Madrid have won the Champions League more than any team, but how many times have they bagged the trophy?

3 Which of these clubs didn't play in the Champions League in 2016-17 – Napoli, Bayer Leverkusen, Sevilla or Chelsea?

4 Which awesome English club played in the competition for the first time in its history this season?

5 Which amazing stadium will host the 2016-17 CL Final – Wembley, Principality Stadium or Allianz Arena?

1. *Griezmann*

2. *Özil*

CL◯SE-UP!

Which CL superstars have we zoomed in on?

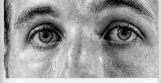

3. *Kane*

4. *Higuain*

SOCCER SCRABBLE

Rearrange these letters to figure out the name of a Champions League legend!

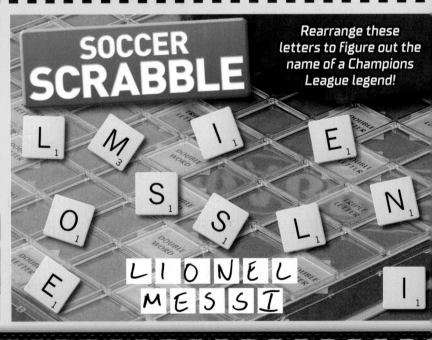

LIONEL MESSI

NAME THE TEAM!

Can you remember the Real Madrid starting XI from last season's Champo League final?

Goalkeeper ★ Costa Rica
KEYLOR NAVAS

1. Centre-back ★ Spain
Ramos

2. Centre-back ★ Portugal
Pepe

3. Midfielder ★ Germany
Kroos

4. Striker ★ France
Benzema

5. Winger ★ Portugal
Ronaldo

6. Winger ★ Wales
Bale

7. Left-back ★ Brazil
Marcelo

8. Midfielder ★ Brazil
Casemiro

9. Right-back ★ Spain
D. Carvajal

10. Midfielder ★ Croatia
Modric

SUPER SKIPPERS!

Who are the captains of these mega clubs?

Leicester
Morgan

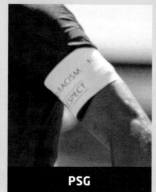

PSG
T. Silva

Bayern Munich
Lahm

Juventus

GOAL MACHINES!

Name the CL teams these lethal stars play for!

1. Luis Suarez
Barca

2. Olivier Giroud
Arsenal

3. Lorenzo Insigne
Napoli

4. Javier Hernandez
Bayer 04

5. Edinson Cavani
PSG

6. Kevin Gameiro
Atletico. M

MATCH! WINNER!

Who scored the winning spot-kick in last season's CL final penalty shoot-out?

ANSWERS ON PAGE 94

WICKED WORDFIT!

Fit 40 Champo League goal kings into this grid!

Adriano
Aguero
Anelka
Benzema
Crespo
Del Piero
Drogba
Elber
Eto'o
Fabregas

Figo
Gerrard
Giggs
Gomez
Henry
Ibrahimovic
Inzaghi
Jardel
Kaka
Kluivert

Lampard
Lewandowski
Litmanen
Makaay
Messi
Morientes
Muller
Pizarro
Raul
Rebrov

Rivaldo
Robben
Ronaldo
Rooney
Scholes
Shevchenko
Simone
Trezeguet
Van Nistelrooy
Van Persie

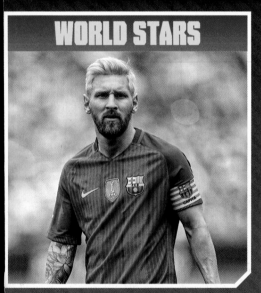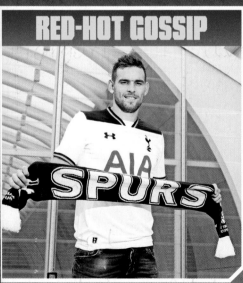

FIRST-EVER GAME
FIFA INTERNATIONAL SOCCER

The original FIFA game came out just before Christmas in 1993, and contained just international teams!

CLUB TEAMS
FIFA 95

A year later, EA introduced club teams for the first time! The Prem, Ligue 1, La Liga, Bundesliga and Eredivisie were all included!

REAL PLAYERS
FIFA 96

Before this game, all the player names were completely made up. FIFA 96 saw real player names included for the first time!

SOUNDTRACK
FIFA: ROAD TO WORLD CUP 98

Loads of changes were made for FIFA 98, but our favourite was the tunes! For the first time, quality songs played in the background while you were playing. Sweet!

ONLINE
FIFA 2001

This change was absolutely huge – it allowed players to go against each other online on the PC!

ALL THE LEAGUES
FIFA 2004

Fans of Football League teams were buzzing when EA introduced all four of England's top divisions!

BE A PRO
FIFA 08

Be A Pro totally changed FIFA as it allowed you to control one player. It later led to Pro Clubs and Player Career Mode, too!

ULTIMATE TEAM
FIFA 09

Where would we be without Ultimate Team? EA included the epic game mode as an extension in FIFA 09 - one of their best ideas ever!

THE AGES

CAREER MODE
FIFA 11

Career Mode made managing your club more realistic than ever. You now had to control a budget and negotiate transfer deals. Plus, if you didn't get results you'd get sacked!

FIFA 11

THE JOURNEY
FIFA 17

EA's new technology allows you to follow in the footsteps of a Premier League footballer in incredible detail! You're in total control of Alex Hunter's career - not just on the pitch, but his life decisions off the pitch, as well as his interactions with managers, team-mates and the media. The new game mode will change FIFA forever!

DELUXE EDITION

FIFA 17

Football LEGENDS!

ARSENAL

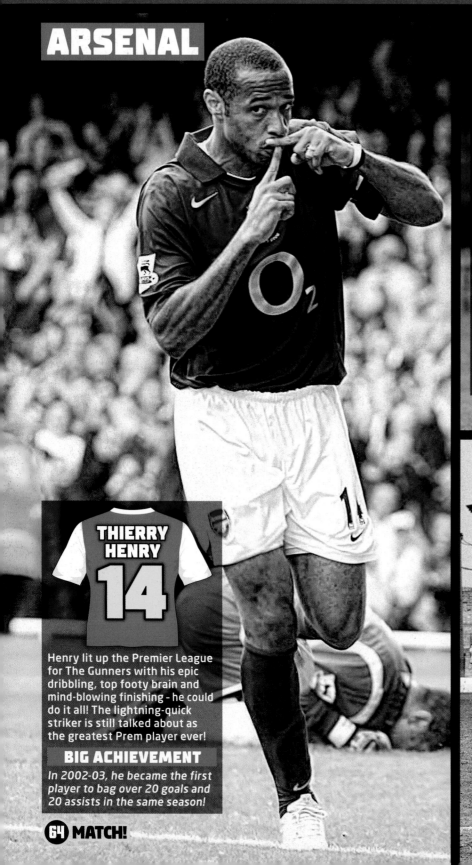

THIERRY HENRY
14

Henry lit up the Premier League for The Gunners with his epic dribbling, top footy brain and mind-blowing finishing - he could do it all! The lightning-quick striker is still talked about as the greatest Prem player ever!

BIG ACHIEVEMENT
In 2002-03, he became the first player to bag over 20 goals and 20 assists in the same season!

BOURNEMOUTH

EDDIE HOWE
20

You might only know Howe as the Bournemouth manager, but as a player he racked up over 250 appearances for The Cherries! He was a classy CB, with a style of play similar to his tactics as a boss - passes galore!

BIG ACHIEVEMENT
Taking Bournemouth from League 2 to the Prem earns him legendary status at the club!

BURNLEY

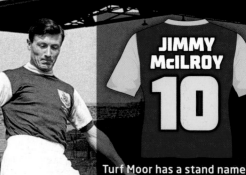

JIMMY McILROY
10

Turf Moor has a stand named after McIlroy - that shows how much of a Clarets legend he is! He was a skilful dribbler, could play as a CAM or forward and had an eye for goal - he ripped over 130 nets for Burnley!

BIG ACHIEVEMENT
The goal king was part of the last Burnley side to win the top tier of English footy in 1959-6

CHELSEA

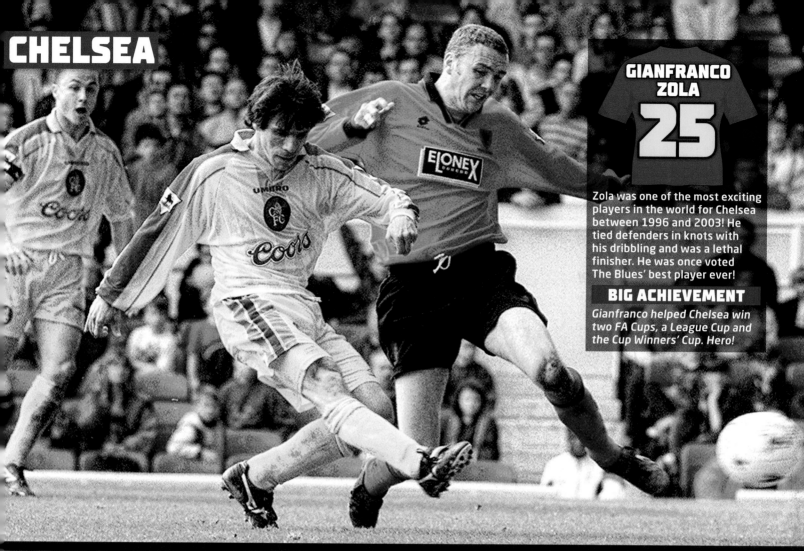

CRYSTAL PALACE

EVERTON

IAN WRIGHT
12

Some of you will know Wright as an Arsenal legend, but he was ripping tons of nets for The Eagles before he moved to The Gunners! The lethal finisher hit 117 goals in six Selhurst seasons – only two players have more!

BIG ACHIEVEMENT

Wright scored 33 goals in all comps as Palace won promotion to the top flight in 1988-89!

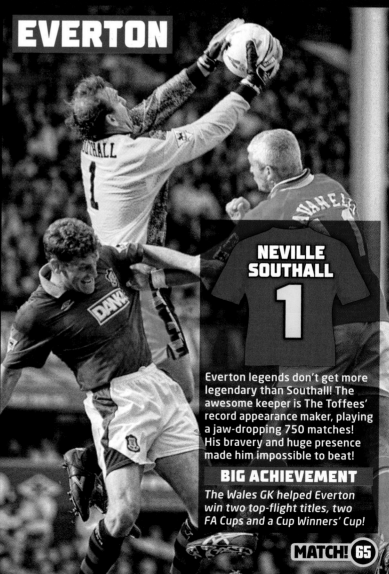

NEVILLE SOUTHALL
1

Everton legends don't get more legendary than Southall! The awesome keeper is The Toffees' record appearance maker, playing a jaw-dropping 750 matches! His bravery and huge presence made him impossible to beat!

BIG ACHIEVEMENT

The Wales GK helped Everton win two top-flight titles, two FA Cups and a Cup Winners' Cup!

HULL

DEAN WINDASS
9

Windass played for tons of clubs, but he's most famous for his time at hometown club Hull. He was a bulldozer of a striker, with mega strength and huge power shots! He played over 250 times for The Tigers, scoring 89 goals!

BIG ACHIEVEMENT

He hit an epic volley in the 2008 Play-Off Final to seal Hull's first ever promotion to the Prem!

LEICESTER

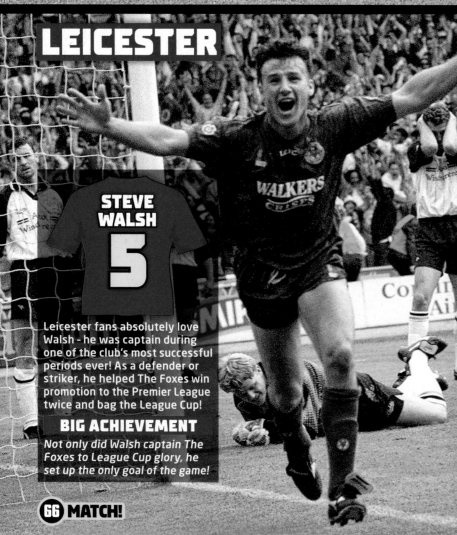

STEVE WALSH
5

Leicester fans absolutely love Walsh - he was captain during one of the club's most successful periods ever! As a defender or striker, he helped The Foxes win promotion to the Premier League twice and bag the League Cup!

BIG ACHIEVEMENT

Not only did Walsh captain The Foxes to League Cup glory, he set up the only goal of the game!

LIVERPOOL

MAN. CITY

SHAUN GOATER 10

City fans used to chant, 'Feed The Goat and he will score', and they weren't lying - the wicked hitman bagged over 100 times for the club! His strength, energy and finishing skills made him a nightmare for defenders!

BIG ACHIEVEMENT

Goater became the first City player in 30 years to score 30 goals in a season in 2001-02!

MAN. UNITED

ERIC CANTONA 7

'King Eric' was the player who started United's domination of the early Prem era, winning four of the first five league titles! He oozed class and scored goals out of nothing. With his collar up, there was no stopping Cantona!

BIG ACHIEVEMENT

Eric captained United to FA Cup glory in 1996, scoring the winner in the final against Liverpool!

KENNY DALGLISH 7

...glish must have a big trophy ...inet - he won tons of the ...ngs at Anfield! The goal king ...yed, and later managed, The ...s between 1977 and 1991 ... picked up a huge 27 trophies, ...uding three European Cups!

...IG ACHIEVEMENT

...ired The Reds to their second ...r European Cup, scoring the ...ner in the 1978 final. Hero!

MIDDLESBROUGH

JUNINHO 10

If you looked up Samba star in the MATCH footy dictionary, Juninho would be staring right back at you! His eye-catching runs and ace finishing lit up The Riverside in the '90s - defenders couldn't get near the CAM!

TOP ACHIEVEMENT

The little magician was part of the Middlesbrough team that won the League Cup in 2004!

SOUTHAMPTON

MATT LE TISSIER
7

They don't make players like Le Tiss any more! The one-club man is Mr. Southampton, playing over 500 times for them. He used to walk - yep, we said walk - past players, and would only score mind-blowing wondergoals!

BIG ACHIEVEMENT

In 1994-95, the CAM was in the Prem Team Of The Year and won the Goal Of The Season award!

STOKE

STANLEY MATTHEWS
7

When Matthews ran with the ball, it looked like it was glued to his feet - it's no surprise he was nicknamed 'The Wizard Of The Dribble'! He played over 350 games for The Potters, playing until he was 50. That's crazy!

BIG ACHIEVEMENT

Matthews still holds the record for being the oldest player to ever play in the top flight!

JIMMY GREAVES
8

Greaves was the ultimate goal machine - he scored 266 goals in 379 games for Spurs, and hit over 20 league goals in seven of his nine seasons at White Hart Lane! He's also England's fourth highest goalscorer of all time!

BIG ACHIEVEMENT

No-one has ripped more nets in the history of English top-flight footy than Greaves - 357 goals!

SUNDERLAND

KEVIN PHILLIPS
10

Phillips hit 61 Premier League goals for Sunderland - that's nearly double the total of any other Black Cats star! King Kev's famous for being a penalty-box predator, but he did score the odd long-range worldy too!

BIG ACHIEVEMENT

Phillips bagged the Prem Golden Boot and European Golden Shoe in 1999-2000. Total ledge!

SWANSEA

LEE TRUNDLE 10

Trundle has a ridiculous scoring record for The Swans - 91 goals in 194 games is nearly a goal every other match! The skilful striker once had a section in MATCH called 'Trundle's Tricks', too - that's how good he was!

BIG ACHIEVEMENT

The lethal lefty's 22 goals in the 2004-05 season helped Swansea win promotion to League 1!

TOTTENHAM

WATFORD

LUTHER BLISSETT 8

Nobody's scored more goals or played more games for Watford than Blissett - now that's what you call a proper legend! His net busting skills fired The Hornets from the fourth tier to the top flight between 1978 and 1982!

BIG ACHIEVEMENT

While a Watford player in 1982, he scored a hat-trick on his full international debut for England!

WEST BROM

JEFF ASTLE 9

Known as 'The King', Astle was a real heading hero! The lethal hitman was unbeatable in the air, netting 174 goals for The Baggies in a ten-year career at The Hawthorns! He had huge power shots in his locker, too!

BIG ACHIEVEMENT

In the 1968 FA Cup Final, Astle scored the only goal of the game to bag the cup for West Brom!

WEST HAM

BOBBY MOORE 6

Bobby Moore is most famous for captaining England to World Cup glory in 1966, but his club career for West Ham was just as mega! He played 644 times for the club and is considered one of the greatest defenders ever!

BIG ACHIEVEMENT

The class centre-back led the The Hammers to FA Cup glory in 1964, beating Preston 3-2!

SNAPPED!
BEST OF 2016! PART TWO

Bonkers superstition!

Howard licks the post before every game!

MMMM, TASTES LIKE BUBBLEGUM!

Musical statues!

Deeney takes games well seriously!

NOW FREEZE!

Valdes' stink bomb!

Job swap!

Is Cavani a WWE guest referee?

ONE, TWO, THREE!

Dortmund's Dynamo!

Magician Dynamo has nothing on Aubameyang!

I CAN LEVITATE FOR HOURS!

Busted!

Williams' headers are lethal!

GET ME A PUMP!

Allardyce shows off his moves!

WHOAH... STAND CLEAR, EVERYONE!

Stroppy Soldado!

HOW DARE YOU BOOK ME!

RED FOR BAD BREATH IF YOU CARRY ON!

WHEN YOU GOTTA GO, YOU GOTTA GO!

Roberto Parp-inez?

Is Martinez sitting on an imaginary toilet?

BIG MATCH! QUIZ

LA LIGA SPECIAL

Zidane Simeone Poyet

CAMERA SHY!

Can you name the awesome gaffers hiding from the MATCH snapper?

crazy names!

Which La Liga clubs have these nicknames?

1. The Mattressers

2. The Yellow Submarine

3. The Meringues

4. The Lions

5. The Royals

6. The Big Greens
Betis

LA LIGA HEROES!

A VALENCIA C.F.
Valencia

B FCB
Barcelona

C
Atletico Madrid

Andre Gome
1

Jose Gaya
2

Diego Godir
3

Match these La Liga megastars to the clubs they play for!

TRUE or FALSE?

Read these statements and work out if they're true or false!

1. Barcelona did the double over Real Madrid in the 2015-16 league season!

2. La Liga giants Deportivo were relegated from La Liga last season!

3. Karim Benzema was the top-scoring Frenchman in the 2015-16 season!

4. There are 18 teams in La Liga!

5. Real Madrid and Barcelona have won more La Liga titles than the rest of the league put together!

MYSTERY MASCOT!

Use the clues to work out which La Liga club this mascot is from!

↘ My team's nickname is The Bats, and I fly aroun the Mestalla Stadium!

↘ For most of last seaso my team had an English boss, but he got sacked!

↘ I cheer on stars like Ga Parejo and Abdennour!

Valencia

Dream Team!

Can you work out which players are in MATCH's La Liga XI?

GK — Slovenia keeper who played in the 2016 CL Final!
Oblak

RB — Atletico Madrid and Spain's first choice right-back!
Juanfran

CB — Barcelona's summer signing from Lyon!
Umtiti

CB — Classy Athletic Bilbao wonderkid from France!
Laporte

LB — Full-back for both Real Madrid and Brazil!
Marcelo

RM — Valencia's new trickster that won Euro 2016!
Nani

CM — Real Madrid's midfield maestro from Croatia!
Modric

CM — Sevilla's ex-Stoke defensive midfielder!
N'zonzi

LM — Atletico Madrid and Spain creative king!
Koke

ST — Villarreal's experienced ex-Spurs striker!
Soldado

ST — Ancient Athletic Bilbao and Spain target man!
Aduriz

the PRICE iS Right!

Match the stars with the money their current club paid for them!

1. Denis Suarez — Barcelona
2. Kevin Gameiro — Atletico
3. Alvaro Morata — Real Madrid
4. W. Ben Yedder — Sevilla

A. £23.4 million
B. £7.8 million
C. £2.7 million
D. £28 million

BEARD SPOTTER!

Which La Liga stars forgot to shave this morning?

 1. Carvajal

 2. Negredo

 3. Messi

 4. Carrasco

DERBY RIVALS!

Match up the two teams who call each other 'The Enemy!'

1. Athletic Bilbao
2. Real Madrid
3. Sevilla
4. Barcelona

A. Real Sociedad
B. Real Betis
C. Espanyol
D. Atletico

CRAZY KIT!

Which team wore this green striped shirt last season?

Betis

ANSWERS ON PAGE 94

BIG '10

Do you think you're a La Liga expert? Well, test your Spanish footy knowledge with this rock-solid quiz!

1 Which La Liga team won their fifth Europa League trophy back in May 2016?

2 Swansea striker Borja Baston spent last season on loan at which La Liga club?

3 Which team has won La Liga more than any other club?

4 Which player holds the record for the most La Liga hat-tricks ever?

5 Sunderland manager David Moyes spent 12 months in charge of which wicked Spanish club?

6 Who finished as Atletico Madrid's top goalscorer in the 2015-16 season?

7 Who is the 'Pichichi' award given to at the end of every La Liga season - the best gaffer, top goalscorer, best goalkeeper or Young Player Of The Year?

8 Only three teams have played in every La Liga season - Real Madrid, Barça and which other side?

9 True or False? Lionel Messi won his first La Liga Player Of The Month award in January 2016!

10 The Mestalla is the home of which Spanish club?

ANSWERS ON PAGE 94

MATCH!
THE BEST FOOTBALL MAGAZINE!

POGBA

STAT ATTACK

Nobody bagged more Serie A assists in 2015-16 than football's most expensive player ever!

BOOTS

Adidas ACE 16+

FIFA 17
TRICK

THE SPIN
Push the right stick diagonally

ANGEL DI MARIA

ROUTE TO THE THRONE

Since Zlatan Ibrahimovic joined Man. United, Ligue 1 has needed a new king – and Di Maria has picked up the crown! The Argentina ace was a key man as PSG bossed 2015-16, and his creativity and pace will help them rule 2017 too!

67

Between 2011-12 and 2015-16, Di Maria got 67 league assists!

ROYAL MOMENTS!

GOLD MEDALIST

Di Maria is a hero to Argentina fans after playing a key role in their 2008 Olympics victory. The speed demon bagged the winner in the quarters, then sealed gold with a beautiful chipped finish in the final!

CL LEGEND

ADM proved himself as a real world-class talent in the 2014 Champions League Final! The dynamite dribbler was named Man Of The Match as his team won their tenth CL title. He didn't stop running all game!

2015-16 STATS

Games	29
Goals	10
Assists	18
Chances created	98

£152.15 MILLION

Di Maria is the most expensive player in football history when it comes to combined transfer fees!

TROPHY CABINET

Portuguese Primeira Liga: 2009-10
Portuguese League Cup: 2008-09, 2009-10
Champions League: 2013-14
La Liga: 2011-12
Copa del Rey: 2010-11, 2013-14
Spanish Super Cup: 2012
UEFA Super Cup: 2014
Ligue 1: 2015-16
French Cup: 2015-16
French League Cup: 2015-16
French Community Shield: 2016

WEAPONS ARMOURY

✓ Ace Acceleration
✓ Quality Creativity
✓ Endless Energy

LIGUE 1 WINNER

In his first season in France, Di Maria ruled! The Argentine bagged a record 18 assists and was selected in the Team Of The Season as PSG won their fourth consecutive title by a whopping 31 points!

FRENCH CUP KING

Angel finished his debut season with two more trophies! He was PSG's top scorer in the French League Cup, then bagged an assist in the French Cup final as PSG did the domestic treble!

WORLD'S RICHEST

£15 MILLION

ANGEL DI MARIA
PSG

Wages: £13.5 million
Sponsorship: £1.5 million

Di Maria might have flopped big-time in the Premier League with Man. United, but that didn't stop PSG making him one of the highest earners on the planet! Only Thiago Silva earns more than the Argentina winger in Ligue 1!

£15.5 MILLION

BASTIAN SCHWEINSTEIGER
MAN. UNITED

Wages: £13.5 million
Sponsorship: £2 million

The ex-Germany captain also had a dodgy spell at United, but his legendary reputation bagged him a big contract in 2015-16! A deal with Adidas and starring in ads for Beats By Dre beefed up his earnings by a cool £2 million!

LUIS SUAREZ
BARCELONA

Wages: £12.5 million
Sponsorship: £4 million

Suarez had the best goals-to-pay ratio of any player on this list in 2015-16 – he bagged an epic 59 goals in all comps for Barcelona! Starring in Pepsi ads and being one of Adidas' main faces boosted his wealth by another £4 million!

£16.5 MILLION

SERGIO AGUERO
MAN. CITY

Wages: £12 million
Sponsorship: £5 million

Being Puma's No.1 star, featuring in adverts for FIFA 16 and taking home one of the biggest salaries at The Etihad saw Aguero bag tons of dosh in 2016! No Premier League player earns more off the pitch than the City goal machine!

£17 MILLION

£18 MILLION

WAYNE ROONEY
MAN. UNITED

Wages: £14 million
Sponsorship: £4 million

Wazza's one of the highest earners in the Prem – the United skipper bags £260,000 a week thanks to his monster contract at Old Trafford! That, plus sponsorship deals with Nike and Harper Collins, make Rooney one of the richest England players of all time!

£25 MILLION

GARETH BALE
REAL MADRID

Wages: £17 million
Sponsorship: £8 million

Bale is the richest British footy star on the planet and the second most expensive player of all time behind Paul Pogba! He's also got mega deals with Adidas, Sony Xperia and ZipTel, and is one of BT Sport's main faces for their Champo League coverage. Sweet!

£26 MILLION

ZLATAN IBRAHIMOVIC
MAN. UNITED

Wages: £21 million
Sponsorship: £5 million

Ibra was the highest earner in France before leaving PSG last summer, and now he's up there with Rooney as one of the highest paid players at Old Trafford! He's got tons of deals off the pitch too, with the flashest being his own Zlatan fragrance!

FOOTY STARS!

£26 MILLION

NEYMAR
BARCELONA

Wages: £10 million
Sponsorship: £16 million

The Brazil ledge is the only footy star who earns more money off the pitch than he does on it! He has the lowest wages of anyone on this list, but big deals with Panasonic, Nike, Rexona, Gillette, Police and Beats By Dre meant he got mega bucks in 2016!

£56 MILLION

LIONEL MESSI
BARCELONA

Wages: £37 million
Sponsorship: £19 million

Leo is Barça's top earner, which is no surprise seeing as he's one of the best footy stars ever! That status has sealed wallet-busting deals with Gatorade and Lays, got him on the cover of past FIFAs and bagged him his own boots with Adidas. Total legend!

£61 MILLION

CRISTIANO RONALDO
REAL MADRID

Wages: £39 million
Sponsorship: £22 million

Not only is C-Ron a European champion for both club and country, he's the richest footy star on the planet! He earns more on and off the pitch than anyone, and has over 220 million social media fans - more than any athlete in the world!

Figures from Forbes' world's highest-paid athletes list.

EURO 2016 SCRAPBOOK!

MATCH looks back at the big moments from last summer's Euros!

PERFECT PAYET!

There was big pressure on France to deliver in the opening match against Romania... step forward Dimitri Payet with a last-gasp screamer!

DRAGONS ROAR!

Hal Robson-Kanu's late winner against Slovakia bags Wales their first victory at a major tournament for 58 years!

ELECTRIC ERIC!

Eric Dier made all our jaws drop after slamming an unstoppable free-kick past Russia!

FAN-TASTIC!

Around 200,000 England, Wales, Northern Ireland and Republic Of Ireland fans travelled to France to watch the wicked tournament!

ICE-COLD RON!

Iceland draw 1-1 with Portugal on their major tournament debut, then celebrate way too much for Ronaldo's liking!

LAST-MINUTE LIONS!

GO GREEN & WHITES!

Northen Ireland seal their first ever victory at a Euros with a class 2-0 win over Ukraine!

WALES BOUNCE BACK!

Wales put the defeat to England behind them by thrashing Russia 3-0 to top Group B! Gareth Bale scores his third goal in three games!

Daniel Sturridge scores a dramatic injury-time winner as England come from behind to beat rivals Wales 2-1!

MAGNIFICENT McGOVERN!

Northern Ireland lose 1-0 to Germany, but it would have been a much bigger scoreline if it wasn't for Michael McGovern's crazy wondersaves!

BANGIN' BRADY!

Robbie Brady scores a vital late goal against Italy to send Republic Of Ireland through to the knockout stages!

CRAZY COMMENTATOR!

An Icelandic commentator becomes an internet sensation after going mad when his country score a last-gasp winner against Austria! The win sets up a last 16 tie against England!

ROCKIN' RONALDO!

Ronaldo scores his first goals of the Euros, including an amazing backheel flicked finish, as Portgual and Hungary play out a cracking 3-3 draw!

WALES GO MARCHING ON!

Two home nations go head-to-head again in the last 16, with Wales edging out Northern Ireland after Gareth McAuley turns into his own net!

GRIEZ AT THE DOUBLE!

Antoine Griezmann proves he's the star of the tournament with a deadly double against Republic Of Ireland!

ICELAND STUN ENGLAND!

England crash out of the Euros after a humiliating 2-1 loss to Iceland. Roy Hodgson then resigns straight after the match!

ROBSON-KANU'S CRUYFF TURN!

Hal Robson-Kanu scores one of the goals of the tournament against Belgium in the quarters, beating two players with a Cruyff turn before firing home!

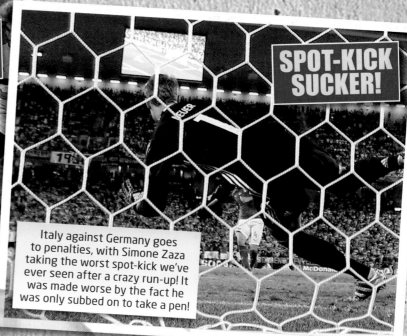

SPOT-KICK SUCKER!

Italy against Germany goes to penalties, with Simone Zaza taking the worst spot-kick we've ever seen after a crazy run-up! It was made worse by the fact he was only subbed on to take a pen!

ANTOINE'S AT IT AGAIN!

Griezmann scores one and grabs two assists as France destroy Iceland 5-2 in the quarters!

C-RON'S THE MAN!

Wales' historic run to the semis is ended as Ron guides Portugal to a 2-0 win over The Dragons!

France reach the final by beating Germany 2-0, thanks to two more goals by Griezmann!

HAPPY HOSTS!

SUPER SUB!

Substitute Eder settles a tense final with a sweet right-foot strike to help Portugal bag their first ever major tournament trophy!

BONKERS FANS!

French jester

Weird warrior

Sick Swede

Welsh burger

Three Lions knight

Bad hair day

Masked mayhem

Green & White Barmy Army

Dodgy dresses

Wacky wigs

Slick shades

Spider-Man fail

MATCH!
THE BEST FOOTBALL MAGAZINE!

BALE

FAB FACT
After signing for Spurs, Bale played 24 times in the Premier League before winning his first game!

STAT ATTACK
Bale scored nine headers in 2015-16 – more than any other player in Europe's top five leagues!

BOOTS
Adidas X 16.1

FIFA 17 TRICK
HEEL TO HEEL FLICK
Flick the right stick up, then flick it down again!

TOP 10 SHOCKING TRANSFERS!

Check out the deals that shook the footy world!

10 ROBINHO
Real Madrid to Man. City
£32.5 million
2008

Deadline day in 2008 was a crazy time to be a Man. City fan – the club got brand-new billionaire owners, then broke the British transfer record to sign Brazil superstar Robinho. No-one could believe it!

9 FERNANDO TORRES
Liverpool to Chelsea
£50 million
2011

Torres was an Anfield hero until he handed in a transfer request to force through a record-breaking move to Liverpool's rivals Chelsea. Unfortunately for him and The Blues, Nando never lived up to his huge price tag!

8 JOHN OBI MIKEL
Lyn to Chelsea
£16 million
2006

Mikel almost joined Man. United before he became a Chelsea player! In 2005, The Red Devils agreed a deal with Norwegian club Lyn, but The Blues said they already had a contract in place with the player. After a year of arguing and kidnapping rumours, Mikel finally signed for Chelsea!

7 WILLIAM GALLAS
Chelsea to Arsenal
Exchange
2006

Gallas was part of the deal that took Ashley Cole to Chelsea, but it was far from straightforward. The defender was so desperate to move to Arsenal, he threatened to score own goals against The Blues if they refused to let him move!

6 FRANK LAMPARD
New York City to Man. City
Loan
2014

Chelsea fans were gutted when their all-time top scorer headed to the MLS, but it got even worse when Lamps joined Man. City on loan a month later! He then scored a late equaliser against The Blues on his Etihad debut. Crazy!

5 ROBIN VAN PERSIE
Arsenal to Man. United
£24 million
2012

RVP finished 2011-12 as the Prem's top scorer and was slowly becoming an Arsenal legend. Once he refused to sign a new deal at The Emirates that summer though, that went right out of the window! A month later he was holding up a Man. United shirt. Traitor!

4 CARLOS TEVEZ
Man. United to Man. City
£25.5 million
2009

Not only did City poach one of the Prem's best hitmen from their local rivals, they mocked United further by putting a pic of Tevez on a billboard with the words, 'Welcome to Manchester'. LOL!

3 ASHLEY COLE
Arsenal to Chelsea
£5 million + Exchange
2006

This transfer saga started in 2005, when Cole was caught secretly meeting Chelsea gaffer Jose Mourinho. The Prem fined him, but he still moved across the capital a year later – earning him the nickname 'Cashley'!

2 LUIS FIGO
Barcelona to Real Madrid
£36.2 million
2000

Barça and Real are two of footy's biggest rivals, so it's no surprise this move made the Catalans well angry! On Figo's return to the Nou Camp, Barça fans threw coins, mobile phones and famously, a pig's head at him!

1 SOL CAMPBELL
Tottenham to Arsenal
Free transfer
2001

Campbell was a big fans' favourite at Tottenham and was expected to sign a new deal when his contract ran out at the end of the 2000-01 season. After months of negotiating, an agreement couldn't be reached, and Sol signed for arch-rivals Arsenal instead!

GONZALO HIGUAIN

ROUTE TO THE THRONE

91 goals in all comps in his first three seasons in Italy... there's no doubt Higuain is the king of Serie A. His epic goalscoring record, which included 36 league goals in 35 starts last season, led to Juventus spending a huge £75.3 million on him. Wow!

64

Higuain is the first non-Italian to score 30 Serie A goals or more in over 60 years!

ROYAL MOMENTS!

LA LIGA LEADER

Higuain played a key role as Real Madrid won the 2011-12 title with 100 points and a record number of goals! He bagged 22 league strikes, and the Spanish giants didn't lose a single game he started!

KING OF THE COPPA

In 2013, Napoli broke their transfer record to spend £34.5 million on Higuain! He repaid the fee by firing them to the Italian Cup final, with a goal in the semi and an assist in the final. Hero!

2015-16 STATS

Games	35
Goals	36
Shots per goal	5.06
Mins per goal	83

£119.85 MILLION

Higuain is one of the most expensive players ever – he's cost almost £120 million in combined transfer fees!

WEAPONS ARMOURY

✔ Lethal Finishing
✔ Aerial Power
✔ Epic Strength

TROPHY CABINET

La Liga:
2006-07, 2007-08, 2011-12
Copa del Rey:
2010-11
Spanish Super Cup:
2008, 2012
Coppa Italia:
2013-14
Italian Super Cup:
2014

SERIE A TAKEOVER

2015-16 was the best year of his career, and he ended it in style! Hig went in to the last game of the season needing to score twice to match the Serie A record for goals in a season, but he bagged a treble to hit 36 goals in total!

RECORD TRANSFER

Still not convinced Gonzalo is the king of Serie A? Well, last summer the deadly hitman became the most expensive player in Italian football history! Reigning champs Juve splashed out a mad £75.3 million on him!

MESSI

FAB FACT
The Barça legend was the holder of different La Liga records before the 2016-17 season started. Wow!

STAT ATTACK
Messi's scored over 22 La Liga goals every season since 2007-08. He's a goal machine!

BOOTS
Adidas MESSI 16.1

FIFA 17 TRICK
SIMPLE RAINBOW
Flick the right stick down once, then up twice!

QUIZ ANSWERS!

Prem Quiz — Pages 16-17

YouTube Star: Daniel Sturridge.

MATCH Maths:
Mourinho Prem titles - three;
Sterling's shirt number - seven;
Add them together - ten.

Nickname Game: 1C; 2D; 3A; 4B.

Freaky Faces: Zlatan Ibrahimovic.

Grounded: Middlesbrough.

Footy Mis-Match: See above.

Wordsearch — Page 18

See below.

FL Quiz — Pages 32-33

Job Swap: Billy Sharp.

Back To The Future:
Adebayo Akinfenwa.

Club Sharers: Wolves.

Flipped: Ross McCormack.

Camera Shy:
Pat Hoban, Glen Rea & Matty Taylor.

Sheff. Wed. Quiz: 1. Hillsborough;
2. False; 3. Republic Of Ireland;
4. Brighton; 5. 27 years old.

Guess The Winners:
2016 - Wigan; 2015 - Bristol City;
2014 - Wolves; 2013 - Doncaster.

Spot The Sponsor:
1. Ipswich; 2. Wimbledon;
3. Fleetwood; 4. Brighton;
5. Coventry; 6. Plymouth.

MATCH Winner: Matt Smith.

Crossword — Page 34

Across:
7. Knockaert; 8. Steven Naismith;
11. Colchester; 15. Forty Eight;
16. Bluebirds; 18. Oldham; 21. Gigg
Lane; 22. Nike; 23. Bournemouth;
24. Hull; 25. League One.

Down:
1. Fourteen; 2. Scott; 3. Three;
4. Northampton; 5. Manchester
United; 6. Neil Etheridge;
9. Grimsby; 10. David Marshall;
12. Blue; 13. Wimbledon;
14. Will Grigg; 17. Scunthorpe;
19. Millwall; 20. Brentford.

CL Quiz — Pages 58-59

Sport Switch:
Pierre-Emerick Aubameyang.

Champo League Quiz: 1. Cristiano
Ronaldo, Neymar & Lionel Messi;
2. 11; 3. Chelsea; 4. Leicester;
5. Principality Stadium.

Close-Up:
1. Antoine Griezmann; 2. Mesut Ozil;
3. Harry Kane; 4. Gonzalo Higuain.

Soccer Scrabble: Lionel Messi.

Name The Team:
1. Sergio Ramos; 2. Pepe;
3. Toni Kroos; 4. Karim Benzema;
5. Cristiano Ronaldo; 6. Gareth Bale;
7. Marcelo; 8. Casemiro; 9. Dani
Carvajal; 10. Luka Modric.

Super Skippers:
1. Wes Morgan; 2. Thiago Silva;
3. Philipp Lahm; 4. Gianluigi Buffon.

Goal Machines: 1. Barcelona;
2. Arsenal; 3. Napoli; 4. Leverkusen;
5. PSG; 6. Atletico Madrid.

MATCH Winner: Cristiano Ronaldo.

Wordfit — Page 60

See below.

La Liga Quiz — Pages 72-73

Camera Shy: Zinedine Zidane,
Diego Simeone & Gus Poyet.

Crazy Names:
1. Atletico Madrid; 2. Villarreal;
3. Real Madrid; 4. Athletic Bilbao;
5. Real Sociedad; 6. Real Betis.

La Liga Heroes: A2; B1; C3.

True or False?: 1. False; 2. False;
3. True; 4. False; 5. True.

Mystery Mascot: Valencia.

Dream Team:
GK - Jan Oblak; RB - Juanfran;
CB - Samuel Umtiti; CB - Aymeric
Laporte; LB - Marcelo; RM - Nani;
CM - Luka Modric; CM - Steven
N'Zonzi; LM - Koke; ST - Roberto
Soldado; ST - Aritz Aduriz.

The Price Is Right: 1C; 2D; 3A; 4B.

Beard Spotter:
1. Dani Carvajal; 2. Kiko Casilla;
3. Lionel Messi; 4. Yannick Carrasco.

Derby Rivals: 1A; 2D; 3B; 4C.

Crazy Kit: Real Betis.

Big 10 — Page 74

1. Sevilla; 2. Eibar; 3. Real Madrid;
4. Cristiano Ronaldo; 5. Real
Sociedad; 6. Antoine Griezmann;
7. The top goalscorer; 8. Athletic
Bilbao; 9. True; 10. Valencia.

*Give yourself one point
for each correct answer!*

SCORE /241